PRAISE FOR TRANSFO PROCUREMENT

I enjoyed reading Janice Marquardt's book *Transform Procurement: The Value of E-Auctions.* Her insights and expertise shine through as she speaks to the need for buy-in from internal users for e-auctions and how she highlights that suppliers can benefit from e-auctions, too. Further, she shares little-known pieces of knowledge like being able to e-auction features other than price. As Janice states in the book, let her past e-auction failures and SUCCESSES help you as you go down the e-auction path to deliver procurement value for your organization.

DR. PETER RALSTON, ASSOCIATE PROFESSOR OF SUPPLY CHAIN MANAGEMENT AT IOWA STATE UNIVERSITY

———

Having been involved in the e-auction business for close to a decade, this book is an extremely valuable resource whether you're new to e-auctions or experienced. It is full of practical takeaways that you can start implementing immediately into your e-auction practices.

LEWIS BARNARD, FOUNDER OF THE MARKETDOJO E-AUCTION COMMUNITY AND BUSINESS DEVELOPMENT LEAD

———

Janice Marquardt's *Transform Procurement* is a masterclass in transforming procurement practices through ethical, strategic, and human-centric e-auction implementation. Drawing from her decade-long journey coordinating over 2,400 e-auctions annually, Marquardt dismantles the myth that e-auctions are inherently adversarial, instead positioning them as catalysts for transparency, innovation, and sustainable supplier relationships. This book is not just a guide—it's a manifesto for procurement leaders ready to reclaim negotiation as a collaborative, value-driven process.

DR. MUDDASSIR AHMED, SUPPLY CHAIN
EXPERT AND FOUNDER OF SCMDOJO

TRANSFORM PROCUREMENT

THE VALUE OF E-AUCTIONS

JANICE MARQUARDT

Red Thread Publishing LLC. 2025

Write to **info@redthreadbooks.com** if you are interested in publishing with Red Falcon Press. Learn more about publications or foreign rights acquisitions of our catalog of books: www.redthreadbooks.com

Paperback ISBN: 979-8-89294-023-8

Ebook ISBN: 979-8-89294-024-5

HardCover ISBN: 979-8-89294-025-2

Cover Design: Red Thread Designs

Author Photo: Jayme Peters, Storyteller Collective Photo Co

CONTENTS

This book is dedicated to Joe Moore,
the best mentor and leader I have ever known.

FOREWORD

I met Janice through a mutual friend and colleague when she was first starting her own business helping companies implement e-auction programs. I immediately enjoyed our chemistry and energy together around our mutual love of auctions. Both of us still get chills every time a customer runs their first auction and begins their journey to saving time and adding value.

Over twenty-five years ago I was hired by GE with zero product development experience, solely for them to be able to pick my brain on how a procurement professional worked. We whiteboarded my methods for negotiating traditional categories and manually mapped out processes before automating them. I spent a full month on the phone with battery suppliers refining and negotiating their bids before the internet or even email. As we worked through different categories, we came up with solutions for scenarios as they arose. Having a mix of domestic vs. international suppliers with different lead times and trade tariffs required implementing bid transformation. The need to give suppliers more time in an active e-auction led to overtime rules.

We had to decide what was and was not visible to suppliers, what kind of notifications and alerts to send, and what type of auction to run. Early auctions at GE were not electronic at all, but instead required suppliers to come to a rotunda in Erie, Pennsylvania to write their bid changes on a clipboard. At the beginning, these events took all day as the suppliers would each have 15 minutes to bid down or pass before retreating into their secluded offices at the edge of the rotunda. Over time these events compressed until they only took an hour, but they were still in person.

After GE, I moved to FreeMarkets where I built a self-service e-auction product called Quick Source. This was the first truly commercial success in a very crowded market that included solutions from Perfect Commerce, Frictionless, MOAI, B2E Market, Commerce One, Procuri, FreeMarkets, Ariba, Iasta, Emptoris, and Bravo. We were mailing CDs to suppliers to install software so they could participate in e-auctions. The traits of a successful e-auction program, now outlined by the book in your hands, showed up even in those early days. Allow me to tell you the tale of two companies.

Both companies in this story were in the boom-and-bust oil and gas industry, were a similar size, and were headquartered in Europe. They both had e-auction programs, yet one was in the top 5% for number of events, savings, adoption, and utilization. The other was in the bottom 5%, and it all came down to leadership, rewards, and recognition. The CEO of the top company sent a letter to all suppliers explaining that e-auctions were how they would conduct all negotiations going forward. Employee bonuses were tied to the success of the e-auction program. The top company provided training in e-auctions with real, hands-on projects. They also ran fun contests between buyers including who could run the smallest or largest e-auction, who could get the greatest savings, and which region internally ran the most spend through e-auctions. Prizes for these contests included a night on the town, prime parking spots in the company lot, plaques, and banners. They were running around 1000 e-auctions per year. In contrast, the company in the bottom 5% of e-auction programs saw little value and were doing none of these things. Running four to six e-auctions each year, they failed to gain momentum and adopt e-auctions sustainably.

I've seen successful programs where the procurement leader refused to approve purchase orders without an e-auction. Another had post-event emails announcing e-auction results sent to the full executive team. Yet another focused on training their most influential procurement leaders in e-auctions to ensure e-auctions were viewed positively and as "non-geeky." The thing all of these successful programs have in common is buy-in from company leadership and the procurement team. That need for buy-in is the strong common thread running through both my experience and this book.

I have seen e-auctions where the category manager stopped the auction because the savings were too good and the category manager didn't think the supplier could do the work. I've had e-auctions where the bidding went *negative* (the supplier would pay the buyer to keep the business) because it was so important to the supplier to have that customer on their sales slide deck to win other business. I've seen e-auctions for human teeth, cadavers, and chicken manure. We were running e-auctions during 9/11 when we had to pause auctions for days while the U.S. worked through major business disruptions. Through all of these scenarios, the e-auction program is not successful due to the category, the industry, or even the timing. The program is successful because of solid change management and good training in the use of the tool.

E-auction approaches and their tools have morphed over the years to continually make a more transparent, level playing field focused on value beyond price. Current tools can factor in diversity, sustainability, and risk, which are all very important to procurement professionals. Many tools started as auction tools and then added in RFX functionality. Tools developed more event types, better graphing, and even full audiovisual cues (adding a "ding" sound made people *so* happy). In the early days no one would touch e-auctions for categories like car rentals, construction, and waste removal. Now there are no forbidden categories.

In evaluating an e-auction software, look for one that is easy to use, includes significant buyer flexibility, has a visible and even slightly flashy bid console, and provides insightful post-bid analysis. Focus on solutions that require fewer mouse clicks to build and run an e-auction that mirrors as many of your use cases as possible. Every sourcing event is different, and an e-auction tool should allow for those differences.

I'm excited about this book because it really focuses on the things that make companies successful. E-auctions are not just about cost, and there is often a false assumption that a company can simply turn on any piece of technology and it will work without proper training and education. This book ties nicely to my favorite story about a buyer whose first auction was wildly successful. She immediately tendered her resignation because she was embarrassed for having such great savings and expected to be fired for not capturing those savings sooner. Instead, her Chief Procurement Officer apologized to her for not enabling her with such a great tool earlier. He highlighted to the whole team that they would see savings using e-auctions and the blame was on *him* for not giving them this tool sooner.

I strongly believe e-auctions are one of the best entry points into procurement. They teach negotiations, categories, technology, and calculating total value. I agree to disagree with Janice that e-auction programs are best run by a separate center of excellence, but I have seen successful models with every organization structure.

In the tale of two companies, which do you want to be? The one successfully building value, saving money, and increasing the speed of your negotiations? Or the one where an e-auction program fizzles and dies after a few months? The next chapter is the beginning of your success story. With this book, you're on the path to making your e-auction program a powerful force for procurement value.

ROGER BLUMBERG

GENERAL MANAGER, NORTH AMERICA
SYNERTRADE

PREFACE

My first e-auction was a bit of a disaster. Three months after the in-person training by our software supplier, I had completed a bid for marketing materials that was ready for auction. I carefully invited suppliers and held my breath. Despite the second and third place suppliers improving their bids multiple times, they never caught up to the first place supplier and the e-auction didn't result in any change to the award. To make matters worse, as a lowly senior buyer I had to present this outcome with a positive spin to a room full of six procurement directors and my Chief Procurement Officer. I didn't manage to get that leadership team's buy-in, which caused a major battle for the next three years. I didn't know how to run a successful auction, how to get the right stakeholders engaged, or how to talk about e-auctions.

Due to an executive decree, my company ran another 27 e-auctions in that first year. I personally ran half of them. The next year, the company created an e-auction team and put me in charge. That year we ran 187 e-auctions. In January of the third year of e-auctions, my CEO got impatient. He decreed all bids for more than $100,000 would use e-auctions as their negotiation tool and that year my team ran 1908 e-auctions. By 2019 we were running more than 2400 e-auctions per year and I had seen every material, service, and category go through e-auction. I didn't have a book to follow and I didn't know any of the experts to ask. While I did not know what an e-auction was on day one, I certainly did by day 1500. I underwent my e-auction journey largely alone, and I am writing this book so you don't have to.

INTRODUCTION

WHY E-AUCTIONS?

In October 2015, I walked into my director's office and told him I was bored. He contemplated me for a moment and responded, "[Our CEO] wants to start doing e-auctions." The regulated utility industry was facing something it had never seen before: competition. While customers still had to buy their energy from a set energy company in most states, they could also put solar panels on their roofs or a small wind turbine in their backyards to replace their energy providers. Rooftop solar and backyard wind created price pressures in a market that previously could raise rates as long as utility boards approved the increase. Our CEO had heard of the fiscal benefits of e-auctions during a board meeting for another company and wanted to capture those benefits for his own business.

The most significant and visible benefit of e-auctions is how they dramatically lower costs—typically three percent overall after conducting a bid but up to 40 percent from the original lowest bid price. My CEO was mainly focused on that benefit. Still, there are others: dramatically decreasing the cycle time to complete bids, increasing the number of suppliers able to engage with bids, creating new markets, increasing information transparency, and generally increasing competitiveness and efficiency in purchasing negotiations.

There are also drawbacks to e-auctions, including the potential deterioration of trust between buyer and supplier, internal resistance to e-auctions, and more upfront preparation required prior to e-auction.[1] E-auctions had a massive moment in the early 2000s, as many companies rapidly implemented this "new negotiation tool" made possible by online software capabilities provided by companies like Ariba. As the challenges appeared after implementation, many companies abandoned this new negotiation tool entirely. When implemented incorrectly, e-auctions quickly become a race to the bottom without considerations for quality or supplier value propositions. When run correctly, e-auctions are a best-and-final-offer process that is fair, fast, and more transparent.

MY INTRODUCTION TO E-AUCTIONS

I didn't know any of the history of e-auctions when I started. Remember, my conversation with my director took place in 2015— long after the heyday of e-auctions had passed. That's why, at the moment (and having never attended a formal supply chain class), I asked my director what an e-auction was.

"It's something like eBay backward," he replied. So, I did what any reasonable person would do: I went back to my desk and Googled it, reading several articles with titles like "'Reverse Auctions Draw Scrutiny" and "The Fall of Internet Auctions and New Age of eCommerce." I learned that an e-auction (specifically a reverse English

1. Shoenherr, T. and V.A. Mabert. 2007. Online Reverse Auctions: Common Myths Versus Evolving Reality. Business Horizons, 50, 373-384. DOI: https://doi.org/10.1016/j.bushor.2007.03.003

electronic auction) is where multiple suppliers bid to sell a specific good or service to a company by decreasing their prices, and the lowest price wins the business. For example, if a company wants to buy a widget, Supplier A bids $5.00 per widget and is in first place. Supplier B bids $4.95 per widget, taking first place and moving Supplier A to second place. Supplier A can decide to lower their price and take first place back (or not). The process of each supplier lowering their bid continues until all suppliers have reached their best and final offer.

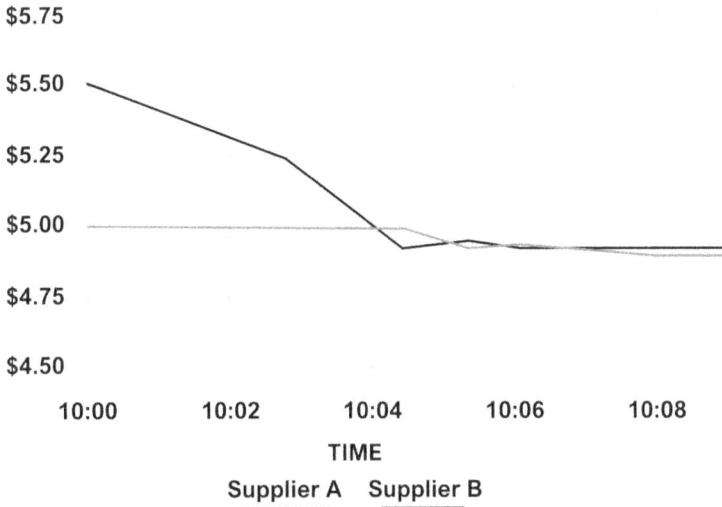

After my first (unsuccessful) e-auction, I continued to learn, experiment, and make mistakes. I didn't have anyone to tell me not to e-auction certain categories or types of bids, so I wasn't limited by conventional wisdom. I was lucky to receive both executive support and the freedom to try different approaches and see what worked best.

WHAT TO EXPECT IN THIS BOOK

This book is not intended to be the definitive textbook on e-auctions, nor an autobiography. Instead, it is meant to guide other companies and professionals by providing practical information on the structure needed to support effective e-auctions, describe why e-auctions are not simply relics, and share lessons I've learned along my e-auction journey to make yours smoother. The journey that started that day in my director's office turned out to be a bit of a wild ride, which I'll also chronicle here because it's a journey in which any company can find value.

As my team started to explore e-auctions and make mistakes, we found a few surprising things that illustrate the value of e-auctions:

- When we used e-auctions as a negotiation tool, they showed cost reductions of 2–3 percent of all spend. That means that for every million dollars in annual expenditures, e-auctions will show $20,000–$30,000 in value. Surprisingly, this value is generated even though approximately *half of e-auctions fail*, producing no savings.
- E-auctions sped up the bidding process. Instead of spending weeks negotiating the best and final offer with suppliers, e-auctions cut that time to minutes.
- E-auctions improved the quality of the scope of work written by our internal customers, which has been one of the best benefits we've found yet. When internal customers know that any supplier who wins an e-auction after a Request for Proposal (RFP) will be their supplier partner, they cannot rely on "our incumbent knows what we need"—an approach often resulting in a sloppy scope of work[2]. Better scopes of work reduce risk by adding clarity, improving communication

2. For more information on an effective scope of work and a sample framework, see Appendix A.

between technical teams, procurement, and suppliers, and reducing change orders or scope creep during projects. While this last benefit is the hardest to measure, it has the best long-term impact on a company.

There are ways to improve all these numbers, including choosing the correct categories for e-auction, using predictive analytics and artificial intelligence to determine more successful bids to auction, and holding the right conversations with suppliers. How do you know if you have a good purchasing category for e-auction? Anything that can get to a bottom-line number can be e-auctioned, including lead time, scope three emissions, or a committed delivery amount based on a set budget. There is more information on non-monetary e-auctions in Chapter Eight, where we discuss next-level opportunities. That being said, some categories are more straightforward to e-auction than others. For example, laptops, tablets, and other IT hardware, are often a great place for quick wins. E-auctions are traditionally used for commoditized materials, but there are also tremendous opportunities just beyond the horizon of nuts and bolts.

As you'll see as we move through the world of e-auctions, the bottom line is that e-auctions have value, that value is fast and fair, and that the right program can improve the opportunity. This book intends to help you set up a program quickly, avoiding the rampant pitfalls and mistakes in the e-auction world.

A BRIEF E-AUCTION HISTORY

In 1994, Glen Meakem was working at GE and came up with the idea of using software to allow suppliers to compete for business in real time[3]. This is right around the time the internet became publicly

---

3. Gorm Larsen, Jacob. 2021. A Practical Guide to E-auctions for Procurement. London: Kogan Page Limited. p. 18. ISBN 978-1-3986-0028-7.

available[4], although early e-auctions were still sometimes conducted by phone or even by mailing floppy disks back and forth. GE rejected Meakem's proposal to conduct e-auctions, so Meakem left GE to form the first e-auction software company, FreeMarkets. In 1998 and 1999 after years of building the company, FreeMarkets had clients such as United Technologies, Emerson Electric and General Motors running e-auctions and seeing huge benefits. By 2001, GE had come back around and was conducting their own e-auctions and seeing value[5]. As the e-auction industry evolved from 1999 to 2004, multiple e-auction software start-ups appeared on the scene and in 2004 Ariba purchased FreeMarkets.[6] However, many early e-auctions were run as straight-to-auctions without a Request for Proposal preceding them. This led to an erosion of trust and value between buyers and suppliers as companies implemented e-auctions without proper training or quality evaluations. The financial crisis of 2008 caused a small resurgence in e-auctions as companies once again focused on cost savings, but the reputation damage to e-auctions as a negotiation tool was already done. SAP acquired Ariba in 2012, giving Ariba the dominant market share in the e-auction industry for those still practicing e-auctions[7]. Most procurement professionals I have spoken to have a visceral reaction to e-auctions, remembering programs implemented without proper foundations or guard rails. This is why e-auctions are ripe for a resurgence as practitioners seek ways to bring negotiations back into the procurement process.

---

4. Couldry, Nick. 2012. Media, Society, World: Social Theory and Digital Media Practice. London: Polity Press. p. 2. ISBN 978-0-7456-3920-8.

5. Radkevitch, U. L. 2008. Online Reverse Auctions for Procurement of Services, doctoral thesis. Rotterdam: Erasmus University.

6. Tate, P. January 23, 2004. Ariba to buy FreeMarkets for about $493 million. Wall Street Journal.

7. "SAP to Expand Cloud Presence with Acquisition of Ariba," May 22, 2012. DGAP - a service of EQS Group AG. https://www.sap.com/investors/en/financial-news/ad-hoc-news/2012/05/1208945.html.

A NOTE ON LANGUAGE AND BOOK STRUCTURE

A note on language and term usage in this book: First, I was taught early in my career that "suppliers" are business partners and "vendors" sell hot dogs. Therefore, I will use suppliers as much as possible and intend for the term suppliers to indicate a higher level of business partnership than a simple transaction for a commoditized category.

Second, my definition of "supply chain" covers the entire supply chain process from demand to delivery to the final customer. The three main categories I consider in the supply chain are procurement, logistics, and warehouse or inventory management. For companies with complicated outbound logistic networks, logistics would cover the final delivery from the warehouse to the external customer.

SUPPLY CHAIN									
Procurement			(Inbound) Logistics		Warehouse or Inventory Management				(Outbound) Logistics
Demand	Bidding and contracts	Purchase orders	Expediting	Trans-portation to warehouse	Receiving	Cycle Counts	Issuing material		Trans-portation to the customer

While the supply chain world is more complex than this and includes many more roles and steps (demand planning, etc.), the graphic illustrates my intent when I use the term in this book. This book focuses on the procurement piece of a supply chain, so I will primarily use the term "procurement" to describe the relevant internal company team most involved with e-auctions.

Third, there is some debate about using the terms "commodity" and "category" in the supply chain world. I use these terms interchangeably, but the distinction is that a category is a broader term that includes more complex items and, therefore, is not "commoditized." At the same time, a commodity implies a straightforward, well-standardized and non-custom purchase. I will try to use the term commodity to imply simpler purchases with well-defined and standard specifications and use the term category to include commodities and more complex or custom areas of supply chain spend.

There are a few tools at the back of this book to help set you up for success. Appendix A includes guidance for writing a scope of work and an example for using a third-party logistics firm to handle shipping and warehousing. Appendix B provides an example implementation project plan for starting an e-auction program. Finally, the Glossary provides definitions for terms found in **bold** starting in Chapter One.

Now that we've got the housekeeping out of the way, let's get started.

ONE

WHY E-AUCTIONS ARE (NOT) EVIL

Reverse online auctions, or **e-auctions**, get a bad rap. **Suppliers** hate them because they perceive e-auctions as impersonal and only about cutting supplier margins. **Internal customers** hate them because they do not allow for the continued selection of the **incumbent** supplier year after year without writing a concise and complete **scope of work**. **Buyers** hate them because they add another step to the process that takes effort to learn and implement. **Executives** hate them because they undermine personal executive relationships.

None of these have to be true.

THE OLD WAY OF DOING THINGS

Suppliers often argue that e-auctions are impersonal and only cut supplier margins. Considering this pushback, it's helpful to consider how **procurement** teams previously conducted cost negotiations to reach a **best and final offer**.

First, the buyer would call up the supplier with the second-lowest **bid**, and the conversation sounded something like this:

> Buyer: Good morning! How are you today?

> > Supplier A: Good morning! Things are going well. It's Monday, so I'm trying to figure out what my week looks like after being on vacation last week.

> Buyer: I hope you had a great time. Where did you go?

> > Supplier A: We took the kids to see my parents, which was great, but now I'm exhausted.

> Buyer: It's always hard to come back; I have a vacation planned in a couple of weeks that feels like forever from now.

> > Supplier A: Definitely. So, how can I help you this morning?

> Buyer: Sure. So, I've been reviewing the RFP bids submitted, and as our incumbent supplier, we know you do really good work. However, your pricing came in a bit high and is currently higher than another supplier who met all of our technical requirements. Can you do anything to sharpen your pencil on pricing?

> > Supplier A: I can certainly look into it. Do you have any guidance on which items we were highest on?

> Buyer: Not really. It was kind of across the board, and you were about two to five percent higher than another bidder. I'd like to see a revised price from you, as we already have contract terms.

Supplier A: Of course. I'll check with my supervisor and the quoting team to see what I can do and get back to you.

Buyer: Thanks. I look forward to hearing from you!

Two days pass, and Supplier A calls the Buyer back.

Supplier A: Good morning! Happy Wednesday!

Buyer: Happy Wednesday to you as well. We're halfway through the week!

Supplier A: Yes! Hey, I've got some good news for you on your pricing. We can drop our RFP pricing by three percent across the board.

Buyer: That's excellent news; thank you! I'll have my supervisor review it and get back to you with the next steps.

Supplier A: Thanks. Have a great day!

The buyer hangs up the phone and picks it up again immediately to call Supplier B, a new respondent to the RFP that the **technical team** liked. Their conversation sounds like this:

Buyer: Good morning! Happy Wednesday!

Supplier B: Happy Wednesday to you too! How can I help you this morning?

Buyer: Glad you asked. I was reviewing your RFP submission for the recent bid, which looks very competitive. However, our incumbent supplier was willing to come down a bit on their price, and now your price is less competitive. Before I award the business, I'd like to give you a chance to sharpen your pencil on that pricing. The technical team was very impressed by your capabilities and liked what they saw in your proposal.

Supplier B: I'm happy to hear the technical team liked what they saw. I'll see what I can do to improve our pricing. Any guidance for us on particular areas of focus?

Buyer: Nothing particular; it was about two to five percent high.

Supplier B: That sounds good. Thanks for letting us take another shot at it. I'll talk to my supervisor and get back to you.

Buyer: Thanks so much! I look forward to hearing back from you.

And the cycle repeats until the buyer gets a "no" from one of the suppliers in the conversations.

There are a few key things to note about this process:

- This conversation took two to three business days and has not yet been resolved. It is common for these conversations to take weeks and even cause the supplier team to travel to the buyer to speed up the process or try to push for resolution.
- This process is manual for the buyer and requires phone skills that are often less common in our digital age.
- The supplier did not get specific feedback on items they were more or less competitive on; they instead received vague

direction on the bid as a whole. While this may have been a negotiation technique by the buyer, it can result in supplier frustration and may or may not help to improve pricing. The suppliers don't know whether their RFP was the lowest price received, higher than the lowest price, or even third or fourth place by price.

- This conversation with either supplier depends on the buyer's willingness to have it instead of simply accepting the RFP pricing. If a buyer does not personally like their sales representative, they are less likely to make the call, leaving room for bias to enter the equation.

While e-auctions can feel less personal than old-fashioned phone conversations, they are much more fair. An e-auction does not rely on the supplier sending holiday gifts for the buyer to invite them to revise their pricing, and it is less subject to personal biases on the part of both parties. Suppliers without the resources to constantly wine and dine the procurement teams they work with can still get a fair shot at the business. The e-auction approach also addresses one of the barriers to entry for diverse suppliers: a lack of fairness in the bid process, which is frequently invisible. Small businesses may not have the resources or expertise to constantly take the right people in your company to lunch or invest weeks into refining their price. Minority-owned suppliers are at an inherent disadvantage if they aren't part of the group of incumbent, well-known suppliers with their historic relationships and unspoken rules of doing business. All this adds up to invisible barriers that an e-auction program can ameliorate. E-auctions level the playing field and increase the ability of small and minority-owned businesses to compete in the bid process.

And yes, at the point of an e-auction, the conversation is again down to price, but that is not different from the previous method of using the phone and waiting two days for a response. *That* conversation was also about price but had more padding around it.

SCOPE OF WORK ISSUES

A key to running an e-auction that isn't a race to the bottom is to run it after a full RFP has vetted all suppliers for technical ability. All suppliers invited to an auction must be technically qualified *before* the auction, and all must be able to perform the scope of work bid, which is why the scope of work is so critical to the success of an e-auction.

A common practice in established businesses is to continue to award work to the same incumbent supplier with each **bid cycle** because that supplier understands the work needed and is comfortable with the technical team. Even in a company with required bid cycles, this can lead to poorly written scopes of work and complacent suppliers. An RFP with a poor scope of work can lead to wildly varying bids as suppliers underestimate or overestimate the risk. The RFP can become a farce, as the work is simply awarded to the incumbent instead of digging into the uncertainty and risk in the project or refining the scope until all suppliers fully understand the company's need.

The other common scope-of-work issue is when the technical team writes it so that only one supplier can provide the scope as written, such as calling for a particular equipment brand name. I once saw a scope of work where the top of the first page said in bold letters: "ONLY **[BRAND X]** EQUIPMENT SHALL BE CONSIDERED FOR AWARD." The brand name called out in bold letters was one with a proprietary distribution network, where each dealer covered a set territory. Calling out one brand in the scope of work made a farce of the bid and e-auction process. After a political battle involving at least one senior vice president, we removed the brand callout from the scope of work and reintroduced competition.

Procurement's role is to draw out and help internal customers define their actual needs, which do not always match the internal customer's ask. The procurement team must partner with their customer to help write the scope of work so that the requirements are precise, not limited to one supplier's ability and define which aspects of the scope the supplier must meet to be invited to the e-auction.

EXECUTIVE AND PROCUREMENT TEAM OBJECTIONS

In addressing the issue of executive relationships, e-auctions quickly become a very political issue. Executives at your company might have personal and professional relationships with executives at suppliers, which can lead to unintentionally biased decisions. Company executives must buy into e-auctions as a strategy to build company value so they can have the proper conversation with their supplier contacts when those supplier contacts call—and they *will* call. Without executive support for an e-auction strategy, the strategy itself becomes invalid.

In short, how the procurement team conducts e-auctions becomes critical to answering the most common objections identified in this chapter:

- An e-auction doesn't have to be impersonal. Relationship-building happens in the RFP and throughout supplier management and an RFP or auction process cannot be the only time procurement builds supplier relationships.
- An e-auction is not the only path to negotiating price; it is a tool in the procurement toolbox. That tool is often fairer, faster, and more objective than a verbal negotiation.
- A complete and clear scope of work allows e-auctions to provide an **apples-to-apples** comparison between suppliers on price and ensures suppliers are bidding the right risk level for the company.
- The e-auction does not need to add much time; once suppliers are trained, they can go through an auction within 24 hours of the technical team completing their RFP evaluation.

- Executives must understand and accept the value auctions can bring and field the concerned internal and external phone calls that result.

If all these conditions are met, e-auctions can become a powerful tool in the procurement toolbox. In the next chapter, we'll examine how the process works in more detail.

TWO
THE E-AUCTION PROCESS

Before launching into implementation details, gathering stakeholder buy-in, and moving into next-level auction opportunities, it is vital to understand the e-auction process and types of e-auctions. One of the benefits of having started e-auctions more than ten years after it was a procurement trend was being able to thoughtfully address issues with the first e-auction wave. When e-auctions began in the late 1990s and early 2000s, they were usually a **straight-to-auction**, where the buyer conducts an auction without a prior RFP or bid process. The company would release specifications and expected quantities in the auction to a group of suppliers, and the lowest-priced suppliers would win the business. This process quickly became a "race to the bottom" between suppliers, who would cut any quality corner necessary to win the auction. While the specifications often contained quality requirements, buyers discovered the disconnect between the specifications and what suppliers bid too late to change the award. The gap between specification and supplier bid resulted in companies paying more than the final auction price to bring quality levels back up or settle for poor quality that continued to deteriorate over time.

The process for this e-auction approach looks like this:

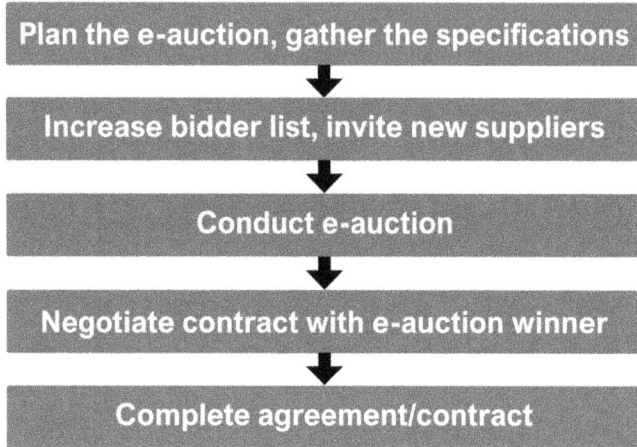

Plan the e-auction, gather the specifications
↓
Increase bidder list, invite new suppliers
↓
Conduct e-auction
↓
Negotiate contract with e-auction winner
↓
Complete agreement/contract

Without an RFP serving as a supplier gate to auction, buyers found it hard to maintain quality control and supplier relationships. The race to the bottom became combative, and many suppliers unwilling to cut quality to compete would walk away from companies using e-auctions as a negotiation tool.

With these lessons in mind, the best practice is to conduct an e-auction after an RFP, which includes a round of technical qualifications.

The RFP before e-auction process is a bit longer and looks like this:

While this approach takes longer than a straight-to-auction approach, the results are more consistent and allow for relationship and quality maintenance. Ultimately, the e-auction does not add significant time beyond the base RFP timeline.

TIMELINE

The best practice is to have a specialized team run e-auctions for a business so they can gain significant expertise in this niche area. While it may be tempting to have buyers run e-auctions as a part of their bid process, this will ultimately take more time and require more training than having a team of specialists. If a separate team is running e-auctions, a sample timeline between completing the RFP evaluation and completing the e-auction looks like this:

DAY 1	DAY 2 OR 3	DAY 3 OR 4
The e-auction team receives a technical evaluation	Practice e-auction, typically in the middle of the day	Live e-auction
The team evaluates the bid for e-auction suitability	Supplier training and conversations	Request cost result breakdown from top 2-3 suppliers
Approval/denial sent to business buyer		Share the result and benefits of e-auction with the business buyer
Set up e-auction (may take longer for more complicated lists of parts)		
Business approves e-auction		
E-auction team notifies suppliers of practice and live auction events		

Note that the process only takes 3–4 days, significantly quicker than a traditional negotiation cycle. While some particularly complicated bids may require more time to set up or run an e-auction, most are best spent in the "Plan the RFP" phase of the overall process. The trickiest part of having a separate e-auction team is managing clean handoffs between the RFP buyer and the e-auction team and ensuring the process is not delayed in these transitions. While the business buyer must know the e-auction process and status, they must rely on the e-auction team's expertise to run a good auction and cannot micromanage the process.

TYPES OF E-AUCTIONS

This book primarily covers an **English Reverse auction**. As a reminder, in an English Reverse auction, suppliers reduce their bids over time until they are unwilling to lower them further. Once the auction timer runs out, the auction ends, and the lowest bid wins. The timer can be extended through the use of **overtime**, which is discussed in Chapter Five.

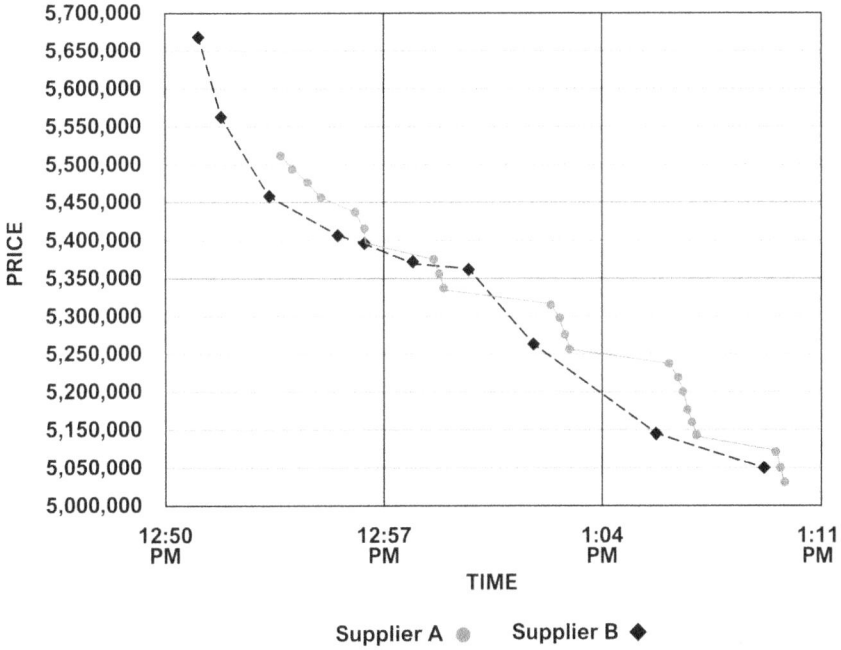

Supplier A ● Supplier B ◆

This book discusses English Reverse auctions because it is the most common format applicable to multiple **categories**. Any bid software package that offers e-auctions will offer the English Reverse type and may or may not offer other types.

———

The second type of e-auction to consider is a **Dutch Reverse** auction. In this type, bids start very low and increase with time. Suppliers watch the bid amounts increase, and the first supplier to accept the current bid amount and enter the auction wins.

Dutch Reverse Auction

Dutch Reverse auctions are very fast because they are complete when a supplier enters a bid. They can be valuable when competition is fierce and the fair market value is well known. Suppliers know at what value the auction ended but do not receive other market data, such as their rank.

———

The third common e-auction type is the Japanese Reverse auction. In this type, the auction value starts high and decreases at set time increments. Suppliers stay in the auction as the bid amount decreases and leave when the bid is at its lowest acceptable value. The auction ends when the last supplier leaves, or a set period of time has passed.

Japanese Reverse Auction

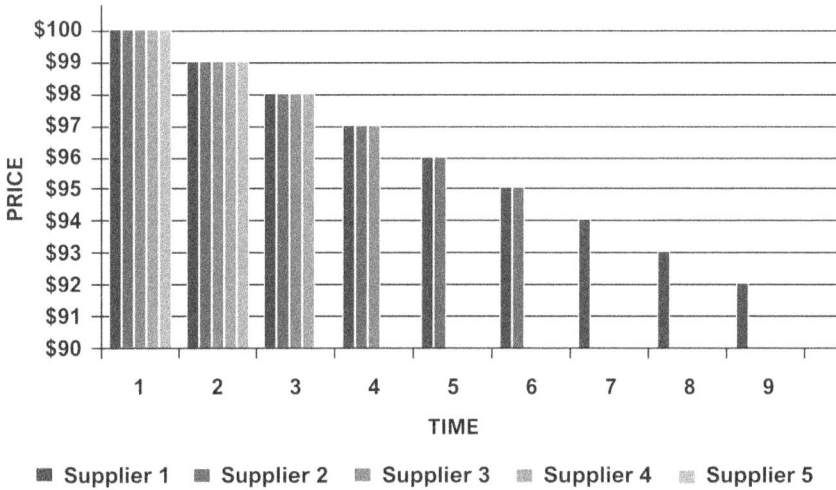

Japanese Reverse auctions are helpful when the buyer is unsure of fair market value for an item, thinks one supplier is significantly lower in price than they have been offering the company, or when the category is particularly secretive and insulated. They can be tricky to understand; they are not intuitive and put maximum pressure on supplier profit margins. Suppliers receive very little market information or benefit from this auction type, making them more likely to refuse to participate.

Now that you understand the most common reverse auction types, the next step to implementation is getting buy-in from key stakeholders. In the next chapter, we'll examine how to do just that.

THREE
EARLY LESSONS

You may be thinking, "This sounds great! *When are we ready to do our first e-auction?*" Let's slow down, as this question involves far more than simply supplier and procurement team readiness. You must consider several other stakeholders and systems.

TAKING THE FIRST STEPS

The required order of readiness for an e-auction program is as follows:

1. Executive team
2. Software capability
3. Procurement/e-auction team
4. Technical team(s)
5. Suppliers

The **executive team** is the first stakeholder needed for an e-auction program. Buy-in from this team is foundational because they will authorize the costs of implementation and software and will message the program's results to a company's board. The executive team usually holds many meaningful supplier relationships and has a deep understanding of the company's values (monetary and non-monetary).

Next in readiness, the **sourcing software** must be capable of running e-auctions. Sourcing software is typically an online platform to move bidding, requests for proposals, and supplier management out of procurement's email inbox and onto a shared host. Examples include Synertrade, SAP Ariba, JAGGAER, MarketDojo, and Coupa, some of the tools to mature a **supply chain** team. Many sourcing software packages have e-auction capability, but ensuring this module has been activated and is available to the procurement team is imperative. If not, the next step is to enable this capability in the software and ensure the information technology (IT) team can support it. At this point, the company should start conversations with the software supplier about the training or support they offer for an e-auction program and decide the level of technical training to start using the e-auction module.

The third group to wrap in is the **procurement or e-auction team**. Readiness for the procurement team includes:

- Understanding e-auctions
- Knowing why the company has chosen to implement an e-auction program
- Training *all* team members on scopes of work that are clear and concise
- Training team members who will set up e-auctions on the software system
- Providing opportunities for the team to express concerns or ask questions

These steps may be easier said than done. For example, I was surprised by the resistance from the procurement team when I first set up e-auctions. One of the teams in my company made the following process map showing our e-auction process.

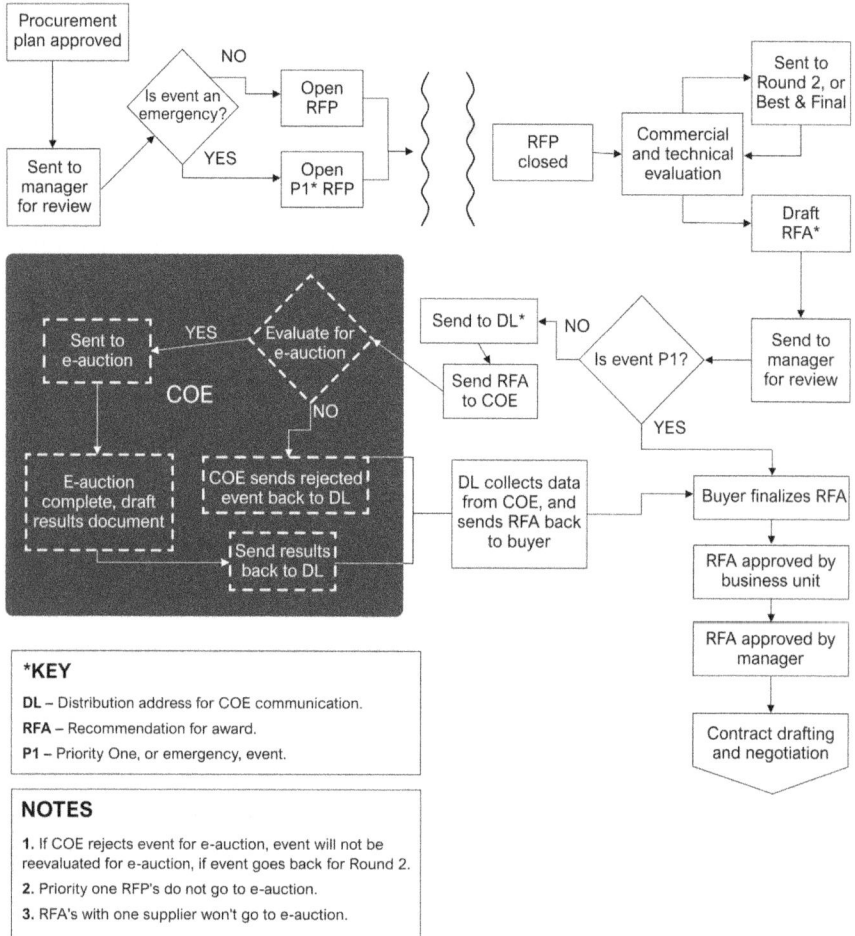

*KEY

DL – Distribution address for COE communication.
RFA – Recommendation for award.
P1 – Priority One, or emergency, event.

NOTES

1. If COE rejects event for e-auction, event will not be reevaluated for e-auction, if event goes back for Round 2.
2. Priority one RFP's do not go to e-auction.
3. RFA's with one supplier won't go to e-auction.

Note the massive "black hole" in the middle of the graphic. It speaks for itself. The procurement team who created this process map viewed e-auctions as a giant black hole, an ugly stain on their otherwise beautiful process. While I had done some work to help my internal customer procurement teams understand what we were doing and why, this process map told me there was still work to do. Getting the procurement team on board is critical before moving on to technical teams.

Once buy-in is established for the executive team, the software is set up, and the procurement team is on board with an e-auction, the next stakeholder group includes the **technical teams**. Getting all technical teams on board with the program at the beginning is often extremely difficult, so the best course is to select key technical teams to start building momentum. The choice hinges on the *people* on the teams much more than the *categories* they need to purchase. A common mistake is choosing categories to start e-auctioning based on what seems easiest or most valuable instead of the internal customers needing to buy those categories.

The best teams to start with are those with an executive leader who is especially excited by the value e-auctions can bring. Other factors for success include having well-written and well-defined specifications for what the team is purchasing and team members having good relationships with their procurement counterparts. The program must build momentum and show value to the first internal customers before the more reluctant teams get on board.

The last group for buy-in is the suppliers engaged in the first e-auctions. An e-auction is often new to a supplier, so having a gentler way to participate and become familiar with the process builds necessary familiarity and buy-in. The training, engagement, and readiness for suppliers occur a little at a time at every e-auction and is a continuous cycle. For the cycle to be effective, it is crucial to have a solid supplier training program (see Chapter Six), contacts within your company suppliers can call with questions, and an opportunity for suppliers to practice participating in an e-auction. Practice auctions help train suppliers and build understanding, allowing them to try their hands at the system in a non-binding environment. It's best to hold a practice auction precisely one business day ahead of the "live" e-auction and invite suppliers to try things they would never do in an e-auction to win business. Examples include entering a bid higher than their previous bid or the **bid ceiling**, entering a bid for $1 or $0, entering bids seconds before the end of the auction, etc. The practice auction timing strategy is vital because you are trying to get your closest possible proxy to the live auction. Holding it a day before helps work out time zone misunderstandings, staff availability and ensures the software and internet are working. Holding the practice auction on the same day does not allow enough time for this kind of troubleshooting. Holding it too far ahead of the real auction provides for too many changes in personnel availability and even weather events.

THE PSYCHOLOGY OF E-AUCTIONS

Early on, I learned that if suppliers can find a way around the e-auction process, they will. Why? E-auctions level the supplier playing field with an objective competition, so working around the process means getting better access to technical teams to try to skew an award, gaining access to more information than the buyer intends to provide, or even sabotaging competing suppliers. Psychology plays at least as much a role in e-auctions as procurement or profit, so to understand e-auctions we must take a little side trip into game theory.

Game theory is an intersection of mathematics and psychology that describes how parties in an interaction make decisions based on the actions of others. Like with a traditional board game, the "moves" or decisions one party makes change how the other parties react. Game theory applies to e-auctions because the buyer sets the "rules" of the game, and the "players" are the suppliers. As each supplier chooses to reduce their bid, the other supplier(s) decide to reduce their bids—or not—accordingly. When all suppliers have reached the bottom bid by which they still profit, the e-auction has attained a **Nash Equilibrium**. The Nash Equilibrium is defined as "a stable state of a system that involves several interacting participants in which no participant can gain by a change of strategy as long as all the other participants remain unchanged."[1] The e-auction ends once a Nash Equilibrium occurs. A side foray into game theory is significant because humans who will do human things are on the other end of an e-auction. Sometimes, that means suppliers get caught up in the excitement of an auction and bid too low. While this happens more often at the beginning of a program, it is typically not sustainable in the long term and will even out over time.

Game theory reminds buyers that the information they share and the "rules" they set can radically change the outcome of the e-auction. Multiple factors—including whether or not the lowest price is visible, when an e-auction can be extended, and even when the e-auction is held during the week—can all affect who wins. Note that Chapter Five has more details on each of these parameters.

The company and procurement team must remember that the long-term goal of a supply chain is sustainability for all parties, which in an e-auction program means suppliers continue "playing the game." An e-auction program is best for uncovering costs previously misaligned to the value of what was provided. Still, using an e-auction program to grind suppliers into non-existence is not recommended. Remember an e-auction is simply a negotiation tool.

Suppliers aren't the only ones who can try to undermine your e-auction initiatives. The next chapter will examine what that can look like from within.

---

1. "WordNet Search - 3.1." Princeton University. Accessed June 5, 2024. http://wordnetweb.princeton.edu/perl/webwn?s=nash+equilibrium.

FOUR
UNDERMINING FROM WITHIN

The biggest challenge in e-auctions is not the software or the procurement knowledge. In truth, the biggest issue—and the most significant opportunity—is always people. The success of an e-auction program is more dependent on how it is understood by technical teams, procurement teams, and executives than on having the best software or knowledge.

TECHNICAL TEAM

Technical teams who write the scopes of work and use the goods or services are the first and last lines of defense in an e-auction program. The technical team must live with the results of a bid and work with the supplier throughout the project, so the procurement and technical teams must be fully aligned for any bid to succeed. Transitions are complicated, and the technical teams are likely comfortable with the suppliers they have used for years. While there is value in having trusted suppliers who know your company and its needs well, a stagnant relationship with little leverage always costs the company money over time. Most technical teams write good scopes of work, but it is often easier to allow an incumbent supplier to write the scope of work or copy and paste a supplier's specifications into a scope. Most technical teams only need to bid their work every few years, and writing a scope of work is not a core skill set for the team. After all, they are appropriately more focused on getting the work done![1]

The bottom line is that an e-auction succeeds best with a clear scope of work, and forcing a technical team to write that clear scope of work is indeed one of the benefits of an e-auction. The best approach is to get one or two technical teams on board with e-auctions who can partner with the procurement team and show what e-auctions can do. Getting key technical teams on board proves the value of the e-auction process to the technical teams who are more hesitant. The most likely first technical team partner at any company is one who:

- Is struggling to meet its annual budget, especially on purchased goods and services.
- Has one or more former supply chain or procurement team members on the technical team.
- Purchases many items that are easiest to e-auction—well-specified materials, IT hardware such as laptops and tablets, or other high-volume and well-defined categories.

PROCUREMENT TEAM

The next internal challenger to e-auctions comes from the procurement or sourcing team. While this may seem counterintuitive, the procurement team has to handle the most change to their processes, the most complaining and concerns from their internal customers and suppliers, and the most questioning of their skills. Most excellent procurement professionals are exceedingly good negotiators with their own methods and practices to complete

---

1. Refer to Appendix A of this book for a sample scope of work you can use as a guide.

negotiations. The e-auction can replace some of that negotiation, so it can feel like the company is trying to undermine the valuable skills those negotiators have carefully cultivated and learned. Let's look at an example of two conversations between a supplier representative and a buyer:

Conversation 1

> Supplier: Hey, I'm calling because I just saw in the scope of work in this bid that there will be an e-auction after the RFP. What's that?

Buyer: Yeah, we have to do this thing where suppliers lower their bids until you can't go any lower or have the lowest price.

> Supplier: That doesn't sound so great. I searched online, and it looks like a race to the bottom. Do I have to participate?

Buyer: Our VP is making us do it, but I agree that it seems like a racket. If you don't participate, we'll use the RFP bids to determine our supplier. You're the incumbent, so the technical team wants to work with you most.

> Supplier: Ok, I'll just submit my RFP bid, then. Call me if I'm not the lowest price in the RFP.

Buyer: Sounds good, will do.

———

Conversation 2

Supplier: Hey, I'm calling because I just saw in the scope of work in this bid that there will be an e-auction after the RFP. What's that?

Buyer: We're trying it out, and it's a chance for you to refine your bid and get a little more information about your price in the market.

Supplier: So other suppliers will be able to see my pricing?

Buyer: No, each supplier can see their bid rank. So, if your bid rank is 1, you currently have the best price. You may need to refine your pricing if it's two or more.

Supplier: I just searched for information about e-auctions, and they seem to be a race to the bottom. Do I have to participate?

Buyer: You don't have to participate; we will use your RFP pricing as your bid if you don't. But then you won't know where you stand in the market. And the fact that we're doing an RFP first allows us to remove suppliers who don't meet our strict quality criteria. That keeps it fair and stops it from becoming a race to the bottom. It's more efficient and transparent than me calling you up and asking you to "sharpen your pencil" like we used to do. Much as I like talking to you.

Supplier: (Chuckles) I used to hate getting those phone calls. I never knew if they were coming or if I would just lose the bid without ever getting a say.

> Buyer: It's true that when I get busy, sometimes it's hard to call every supplier. You'll get a chance to practice this e-auction in the system before we run it for real, and there's a team here to support you through the new process. Thanks for calling and let me know if you have any other questions.

These conversations illustrate the importance of procurement buy-in and how they can undermine an e-auction program before it starts. The best answer to this risk is two-pronged.

- Help these practitioners see the e-auction as another skill in their negotiation toolbox. An e-auction is very good at defining and refining one quantitative thing between suppliers: price, **lead time**, carbon emissions, etc. It is nothing more or less and can be an excellent addition to a versatile negotiator's toolbox.
- Use the e-auction to refine pricing to free up these excellent negotiators for more complicated or qualitative negotiations. Suppose they are not spending all their time going back and forth with suppliers to get the last penny on pricing. In that case, they can spend their efforts refining scopes of work for success, negotiating intangible service items that improve the customer experience, and setting strategies for upcoming complicated projects. An e-auction can remove the "grunt work" off the shoulders of your best negotiators.

EXECUTIVE TEAM

An inevitable phone call is coming when you implement e-auctions that can derail your program if you're not ready. The call is directly from your CEO's golf friend / tennis partner / cousin to the CEO when they get invited to their first e-auction. They are a supplier to the company and have been for years, and they want this new crazy e-auction thing to go away. It is up to the CEO (and perhaps the executive team) how they want to handle this phone call, but it will be much easier if that decision is made beforehand.

In the case of our e-auction program, the supplier who made the phone call was a construction supplier who had been working on our company's facilities and remodels for many years. They were either close friends or cousins with our CEO or his spouse. (I never learned the exact relationship.) My team had included this supplier in an early e-auction, per our process and policy at the time, with nothing unusual about this project. I learned later that the supplier called our CEO directly to seek an exception to the e-auction process. My CEO chose to stand his ground and told the supplier that if they didn't choose to participate in the e-auction, they would not be able to win the business. By modeling the reaction he expected, my CEO made it extremely difficult for any of his executive team to grant supplier e-auction exceptions.

When your CEO or executive team member receives this phone call, their primary response options are:

- Exempt this supplier's category from e-auction. Perhaps this category is a strategic category for the company with few suppliers. This may be the best answer if **spend** is minimal or the company politics surrounding the relationship are particularly tricky. If you choose this approach, consider identifying these suppliers early and preventing the phone call by exempting their categories from auction.
- Tell the supplier that e-auctions are how the company has decided to do business and that if they would like to remain a supplier to the company, they should participate in the e-auction. If you choose this approach, consider reaching out to these suppliers before their first invitation and talking through the supplier benefits of an e-auction (transparency, rapidity, etc.).

Either approach is perfectly valid; again, the vital piece is to consider how you'll handle this situation before it arises.

If leaders at your organization are still particularly reluctant to understand e-auctions, it can be helpful to run a demonstration. Once, at a conference with multiple supply chain leaders, I hosted an e-auction between numerous supply chain leaders where those leaders became our "suppliers." We had them bid on how many seconds they would get to listen to a song to identify it. The "buyer's view" of the auction was visible to the audience, which included members of these leaders' teams. The "suppliers" participated in the auction with the winning bid of three seconds to identify a song in the 1980s rock genre. He did not end up guessing the song, despite his confidence in needing only three seconds, so then the second-place bidder had a chance to listen to four seconds of the music. She also did not get the correct answer, so the third-place auction participant listened for his bid of six seconds and succeeded in guessing "Still of the Night"' by Whitesnake. In addition to being fun, this demonstration increased the audience's and participants' familiarity with e-auctions.

Internal technical, procurement, and executive teams are critical to the success of any e-auction program. While the value will speak for itself, remember that humans are still ultimately emotional, and transitions can be difficult. That's why it's essential to validate, expect, navigate, and plan for the likely issues that will arise.

In the next chapter, we'll examine other ways to prepare you and your organization for success.

FIVE
PARAMETERS AND METRICS

In setting up an e-auction program, there are several technical parameters to configure and metrics to measure success. As with all things in this space, parameter decisions are based more on trade-offs in human behavior than technical capabilities. While each company's industry category may impact parameters, decisions are more based on how a company wants to do business and the level of internal buy-in than any other factors. Bid ceilings, **reserve prices**, and **auction transparency** are external parameters. Categories exempt from e-auction, team structure, and metrics are internal parameters.

Metrics are always important in business and a critical communication tool for an e-auction program. Due to the political nature of e-auctions, metrics tell the story of the program's value to allies and enemies alike. While this chapter lays out some metrics to build the story, the right metrics to measure are based on stakeholder objections. If a key stakeholder says, "E-auction prices are costing the company more than previous prices," measure e-auction price versus **historical price**. If they argue that "E-auctions take too long to run," measure the turnaround time from technical evaluation to e-auction completion.

In short, the best metrics suit the company and identify areas for improvement. Let's explore parameters and metrics further.

EXTERNAL PARAMETERS

The external parameters in the e-auction space are auction timing, bid ceilings, reserve prices, overtime rules, **bid decrements**, tie rules, and auction transparency. These parameter decisions affect the success of an e-auction—or even the entirety of the e-auction program—and all have their share of pros and cons.

The first decision to make in building an e-auction is when to hold the event. The decision is based on supplier geography, company culture, and sometimes even industry. When I was running e-auctions for utility construction, the suppliers were all in the same time zone and had a culture of starting their day early. They wanted to run auctions first thing in the morning, usually before 8:00 AM so they could then go about their day. After participating in the frequent e-auctions, they would know which business they won and be able to spend their day planning for the upcoming work. Other suppliers preferred a later time of day or were in dramatically different time zones. The best times to hold an auction were generally between Tuesday and Thursday, at standard times of day for the industry participating. We did run auctions on Monday afternoons and Friday mornings, but they were often less successful. Running an e-auction on a Friday afternoon or Monday morning is a waste of time and effort.

A **bid ceiling** is the highest possible value at which a supplier may start their e-auction bidding. Some e-auction software allows for different bid ceilings for each supplier, which enables the company to set each supplier's bid ceiling at their request for proposal (RFP) price. Setting individual bid ceilings communicates the price understood as the RFP price and confirms the award price. A bid ceiling can ensure that a low-priced supplier refusing to enter the e-auction environment will still impact the auction result. By having a bid ceiling set at or below the lowest RFP price, the buyer ensures that *any* bidder who enters the auction at the bid ceiling price is a contender to win the bid. It is very frustrating for suppliers to bid down in an auction only to learn later that another supplier's RFP bid was lower than their auction bid.

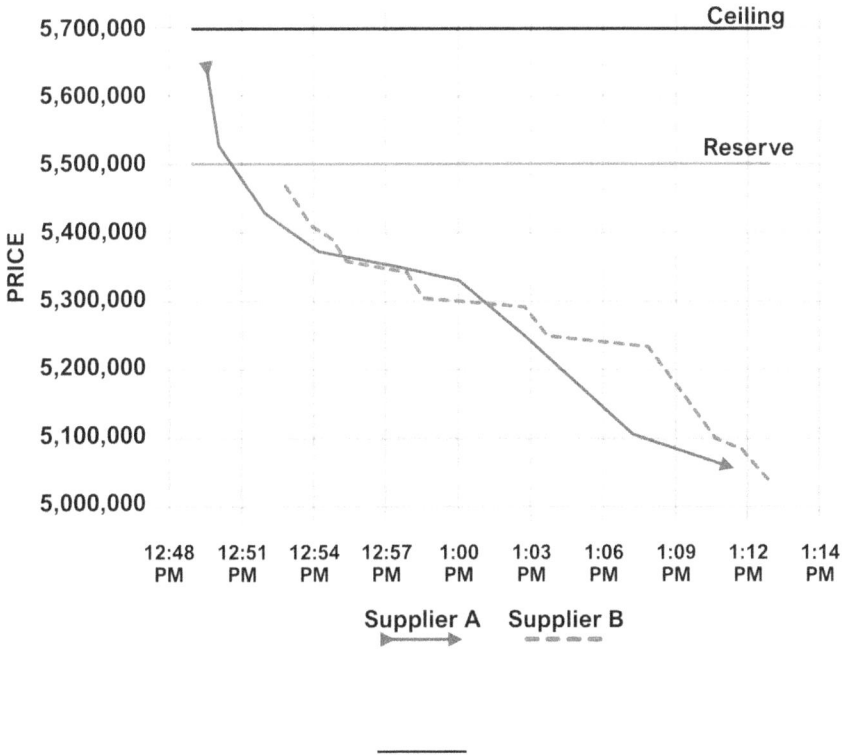

Options for bid ceilings, along with their advantages and disadvantages, are shown in the following table:

CEILING OPTION	ADVANTAGES	DISADVANTAGES
Individual supplier bid ceilings set at RFP price	• Communicates and clarifies RFP price	• Does not put pressure on suppliers to improve price
Individual supplier bid ceilings set just below their RFP price	• Can yield reduction even in non-competitive auctions	• Sends a false message if suppliers come down in price and are not then in first place
One bid ceiling set at the lowest RFP price	• Ensures the e-auction price no more than the RFP price	• Communicates the lowest RFP price to all bidders, which may violate supplier privacy
One bid ceiling set below the lowest RFP price	• Generates reduction if any supplier bids in the auction • Ensures the auction winner wins the bid, even if the first-place RFP supplier does not participate	• Tricky to set a percentage reduction • A consistent percentage below the lowest RFP price leads to suppliers determining the RFP price and may violate supplier privacy
No bid ceiling	• Maximizes the psychology of auctions and competition	• Causes confusion between the lowest RFP price and lowest auction price if the lowest price RFP supplier does not participate in the auction
Bid ceiling set at budget price	• Can ensure the technical team meets budget if it is close to RFP pricing	• An unreasonably high or low budget leads to suppliers dismissing the e-auction entirely

While it can be tempting not to set a bid ceiling, clever suppliers can take advantage of a no-bid ceiling. In an early e-auction where I did not set a bid ceiling, an innovative supplier used that to gain much information about the market. It was a significant bid for a contract of approximately $20 million and had three bidders. The clever supplier started their initial bid at a whopping $70 million. Then, they proceeded to rapidly decrease their bid by $5 million at a time until they reached their RFP price, effectively determining the approximate pricing of each of their two competitors. While I admired their savvy use of the e-auction tool, I learned to set a bid ceiling price to maintain a fairer environment.

A word on using reserve prices: Don't. A reserve price is a price set in secret where the auction is not awarded unless the best auction price is below the reserve price and is more destructive than constructive. Reserve prices sometimes cause suppliers not to bid without knowing the secret reserve price, threatening to destroy the delicate psychology of the auction environment. The primary benefit of an e-auction to a supplier is the added transparency they gain from the process, and *any* removal of openness must be carefully considered.

Overtime is an interesting concept in e-auctions and is much more to the company's advantage than the suppliers. Overtime is when a supplier puts in a new low bid within a few moments of the end of the auction, and the system extends the end to allow all suppliers to consider this latest development. The purpose of overtime is to ensure suppliers do not simply run out of time and are comfortable with the lowest bid they enter. The buyer controls:

- The overtime duration
- Whether the extension applies if a new bid is received in the first or second lowest price or beyond
- How long before the end of an auction overtime triggers

A typical setting is a ten-minute e-auction with an overtime of an additional two minutes if the first or second-place supplier changes within the last two minutes of an auction. Setting overtime with these typical rules means the e-auction will be at least ten minutes long but could last for hours if suppliers continually bid down and change first or second place.

An auction that lasts for an extended period likely says more about the **bid decrement**—the amount the supplier is allowed to decrease their bid—than the overtime rules.

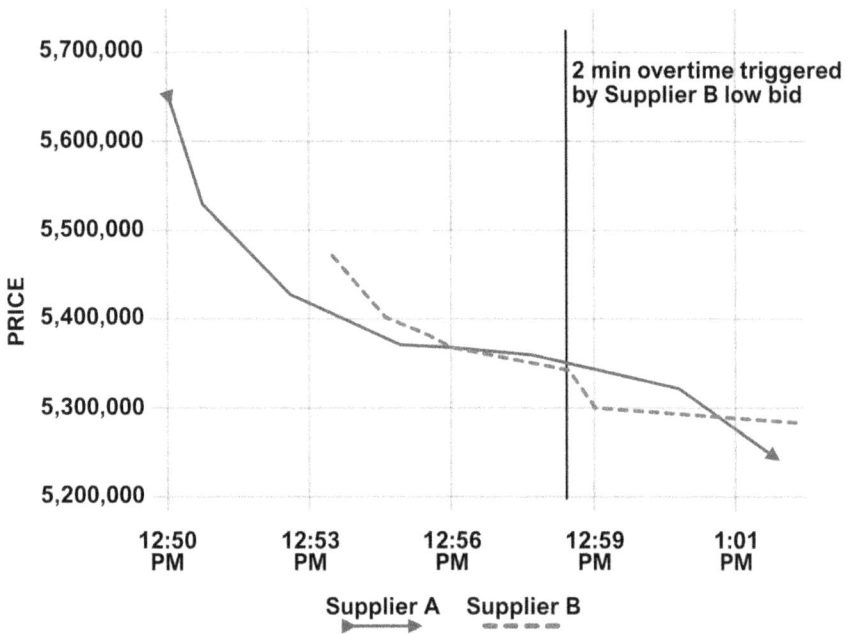

Why do bid decrements work? Consider this: on a bid for over a million dollars, it is inefficient for suppliers to decrease their bids by at least a penny each time. In contrast, it would be disheartening for suppliers to lower their bid by one hundred thousand dollars each time they wished to reduce their price. Typical bid decrements are set around a half a percent of the starting price, with some software allowing the bid decrement to be set as a percentage instead of a set amount. In our million-dollar example, a bid decrement of half a percent means suppliers would need to improve their pricing by at least five thousand dollars with each bid. Auctions that set the decrement too low will last longer as suppliers improve their bids by the minimum amount necessary. Bids with a decrement set too high cause suppliers to disengage from the e-auction, as their best price is above the minimum bid the auction requires and will increase the buyer's final bid.

Once, on a multi-million dollar e-auction for a capital project, the internal customers and suppliers were concerned about their flexibility for bid amounts and lobbied for a small bid decrement. Although the initial bids were around $25 million, we set the bid decrement at $10,000 (0.04 percent). Based on this decision, the e-auction went on for *eight hours*. While the suppliers could bid almost precisely what they wanted on every bid, it tied up their executive sales team for an entire day and may not have even changed the result. Experiences like this leave suppliers and technical teams feeling that e-auctions are a waste of time, regardless of the **cost reductions** or transparency achieved.

As of this book's writing, very few software packages allow for a dynamic bid decrement. A dynamic bid decrement is standard practice in live **forward auctions**, where the auctioneer begins bid decrements for a piece of furniture at twenty dollars and then decreases as the bidding slows to five dollars or one. Some e-auction tools allow a buyer to change the bid decrement while the e-auction is open, but this is a manual process and tricky to manage in real-time. With advances in technology, automatic dynamic bid decrements will likely be possible in the near future.

Ties are particularly tricky in e-auctions. Similar to bid ceilings, tie settings can significantly impact supplier behavior and e-auction results.

Options for ties (not all available in all sourcing software) with their advantages and disadvantages are shown in the following table:

TIE OPTION	ADVANTAGES	DISADVANTAGES
Ties are not allowed; the software rejects bids that would tie	No ambiguity on which supplier won the e-auction	May force supplier to bid lower than their planned floor or stop bidding prematurely
Ties allowed, show both as the same bid rank	Accurately shows a supplier's rank based on bid	Suppliers may think they have won an auction but will not win the business if the company chooses the other tied bidder
Ties allowed, the first supplier, enter the price shows as the better rank	Allows suppliers to enter accurate pricing but does not indicate they are tied so the competition continues	Technical team may argue for the "second" place bidder due to incumbency or preference, seeing the same amount bid, causing friction and loss of trust with suppliers

Auction transparency refers explicitly to what is or is not visible to suppliers within the auction, primarily whether the current lead bid is visible. An e-auction will tell suppliers their bid's rank, but it will not always tell suppliers the lowest current bid unless the buyer sets that parameter. Disclosing the current lead bid has the advantages of increased supplier transparency and a greater understanding of where suppliers stand in their market. Suppliers know precisely how far they need to come down in price to win the business and can make that decision. Auction transparency can lead to better future RFP prices from suppliers who may be unable to reduce their pricing in *this* instance but better understand how to position future proposals.

Disadvantages include the loss of the psychological pressure of e-auctions on suppliers and the potential for disclosing other suppliers' pricing. Chapter Three notes that game theory is an essential aspect of e-auctions. If suppliers can always see the lowest price, they will not get caught up in the excitement of winning the business and will more likely walk away from an e-auction without improving their price. Disclosing the lowest bid makes it more challenging to award part of the business to the second-place supplier because they know how much more the company is willing to pay for their goods or services.

INTERNAL PARAMETERS

The major internal parameters to decide when setting up an e-auction program are which purchases will *not* go through the auction process (e-auction exceptions) and how the team will be structured. Metrics will be discussed later in this chapter, as they are a more prominent topic. As with external parameters, decisions about e-auction exceptions and team structure are based more on how a company approaches e-auctions than on absolute guidelines.

The **exceptions** to an e-auction are hugely subject to company politics. Especially at the beginning of the program, every bid, every technical team, and every potential candidate for auction will assert *some* reason why it is not suitable. As a gentle reminder, e-auctions will typically save 2–3 percent on all bids using them as a refinement negotiation tool from the initial RFP, and about half of all auctions will see no **savings** at all. E-auctions are a volume game, where the value gained is directly proportional to the spend pushed through the process. Therefore, exceptions should be considered carefully. Each company must set its own exceptions list based on the value it wishes to capture, the buy-in from its stakeholders, and the results of its internal politics on the topic.

Note that exemption from the requirement to negotiate using e-auction may or may not mean exemption from a requirement to conduct a competitive bid. Some key exceptions, explanations and examples, and the recommendation of whether they should be exempted are shown in the following table:

POTENTIAL E-AUCTION EXCEPTION	DEFINITION	EXAMPLES	RECOMMENDED TO EXEMPT
Original Equipment Manufacturer (OEM)	Supplier under warranty supplied the original piece of equipment	• Manufacturing equipment repair parts • Maintenance contracts during warranty term • Additional equipment to existing networks (such as radio networks)	Yes, unless the piece of equipment dictating the expansion/replacement is due for bid or outside warranty.
Legal fees, external audits, similar consulting services	Supplier to provide supplemental legal, financial, or audit services	• Financial audits • Litigation assistance • Legal research	No, unless an external party (such as a parent company) is requiring a certain supplier.
Government fees	Fees determined by a regulation or government body	• Fines • Annual business filing fees with state or federal governments	Yes
Software maintenance	Cost to maintain existing software (not implementation or initial license fees)	• Enterprise resource planning (ERP) maintenance • Office or operating system software	Yes, unless software is due for replacement, license renewal, or major upgrade.
Only qualified supplier	Only supplier remaining after technical team disqualifications	• Any time multiple bids are received in response to an RFP, but only one supplier is technically qualified to continue.	No, in this situation, the procurement and technical teams need to work together and reevaluate the approach to avoid the technical team selecting a supplier based on preference.
External customer-required supplier	An external customer requires the company to work with a particular supplier	• A major customer specification requirement has only one possible source, such as due to patents. • A customer requests explicitly (in writing) the use of a particular supplier for their project.	Yes, external customer requests may need to be in writing depending on the procurement policy.
Utilities	Regulated utility purchases	• Water • Electricity	Yes, as long as the market is regulated (unregulated markets are competitive).
Support or administrative services	Human resources, leadership, training, or other support services	• Internal leadership conferences or meetings • Training programs • 401(k) programs	Depending on executive leadership decisions, these can almost always be completed if desired.

As the leader of the e-auction team, I spent hours arguing the e-auction exemption policy with executive and management stakeholders. We did not have a written exemption policy in the early days, and each exemption was up to me to grant. I do *not* recommend this approach because it is time-consuming and burns a lot of political capital. Even after the policy was created, each of my internal customers felt that *their* commodity should be exempted from e-auction, regardless of the documented procedure. Internal stakeholder buy-in is, again, so necessary.

The last significant internal parameter to decide is team structure. How will the procurement team support the e-auction program? While it can be tempting to have all buyers run e-auctions as part of their role, a small e-auction team can focus on running auctions and become experts. Remember, conversations with suppliers, such as the training and support offered to suppliers and internal customers, are critical. Stakeholders need to know they are in good hands and are working with people who understand the e-auction process and are ready to help.

Luckily, one of the great things about an e-auction program is how well-suited it is to a small team and entry-level talent. An extensive e-auction program (at least 2,000 e-auctions annually, or an average of 45 e-auctions per week) can be run by two people once a program is launched. While one person can typically run a program, it's best to have two people to improve supplier communication, make the best use of premium auction times, and simply have someone to cover for a colleague when life happens. You can also add an intern to help cover gaps and start training your talent pipeline. The team running e-auctions sees all different scopes of work and interacts with employees and team members across the company, so it is an excellent place for employees new to the workplace and the company. In addition, e-auction team members can start adding value very quickly once they understand how to build an e-auction, typically within weeks. If you have a phone number suppliers can call for help, the e-auction team learns the customer service skills needed in many roles within a company as they answer that phone and solve problems in real time. All of these build team members rapidly, making them ready for new roles within or outside the supply chain team.

The issue for e-auction team members is that this is a burnout role. They will deal with high-stress, quick timeline demands and often have supplier representatives call with elevated emotions. I strongly recommend moving e-auction team members into roles within the supply chain or elsewhere in the business after about a year and a half of the e-auction team.

I saw the value of the e-auction role when I ran into a former intern on my team six years after he had been running e-auctions. He leveraged his experience running e-auctions into a supply chain demand management role at Apple and has succeeded in that role for over 2.5 years. He did not have a degree specializing in supply chain management, but he had used the learning from his time managing thousands of e-auctions to show his ability in one of the most sophisticated supply chains on the planet.

Together, the internal and external parameters significantly impact the success of an e-auction program. The external parameters such as bid ceilings, overtime, tie rules, and lowest price bid visibility set the tone for suppliers regarding how the company will approach e-auctions. The internal parameters, such as e-auction exceptions and team structure, determine the commitment level and, therefore, the value the company will achieve from the program. Make thoughtful decisions in these areas early to maximize your e-auction value later, and measure this value using the right metrics.

COST SAVINGS AND RFP REDUCTION

Cost savings are often the holy grail that procurement chases. Companies set bonuses, promotions, and metrics based on savings. I have yet to see two companies that measure savings the same way or include the same categories. Are savings the difference between:

- What the company paid for a widget last year versus what they will spend this year?
- The stakeholder's budget and the price paid or contracted?
- The incumbent suppliers' initial proposed price and the price after bids and negotiations?
- Last year's price plus inflation or a commodity index premium and the amount paid or contracted?

I have seen all of these called "savings," although some companies would call them "cost avoidance" and put them in another category. Regarding e-auctions, I prefer to call the benefit e-auctions bring "cost reduction" to avoid confusion.

In the purest sense, **savings** is the difference between what a company paid for something last year and what they paid this year (or have contracted to pay for years into the future). While an e-auction can often generate those savings, the simplest way to measure the benefit of an auction is to isolate the value from the e-auction itself and call it a **cost reduction**.

The cost reduction is calculated by taking the lowest price from the RFP run ahead of the auction and subtracting the lowest final auction price.

In the case of a process that runs an auction without a prior RFP, the cost reduction is the lowest final auction price subtracted from the lowest initial bid received from any participating suppliers.

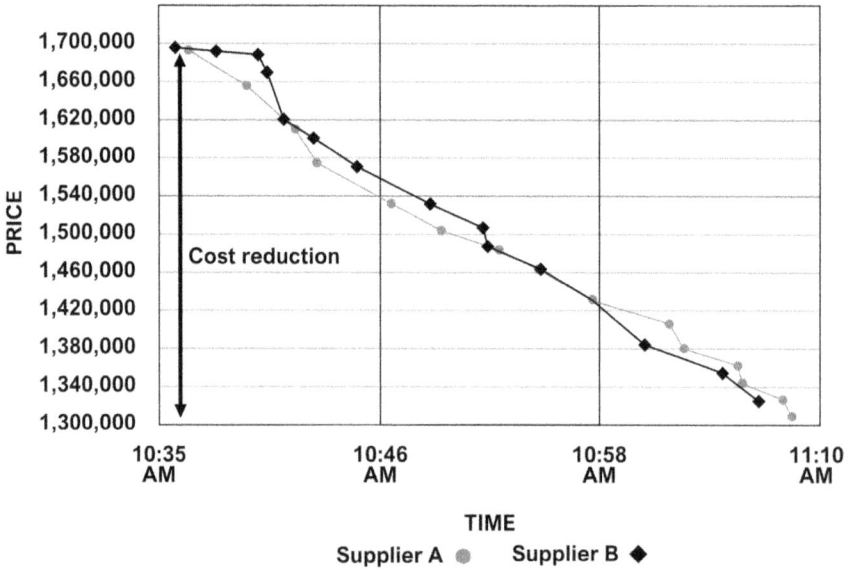

It is hard to disagree that this reduction is a benefit, but it is easy to argue that it is *not* a savings if the lowest auction price is still higher than historic pricing. Measuring it as a cost reduction ensures the benefit of the e-auction is measured realistically but still shows its value.

OTHER METRICS

Some valuable metrics to measure other than cost reduction include cost per auction, comparison to historic or budget pricing, e-auction turnaround time, and the number of suppliers invited to and participating in the auction. Each of these metrics shines a different light on the value e-auctions bring.

The cost per auction is relatively intuitive, but it is essential to counter the argument that e-auctions are expensive to run. Especially if one business in a conglomerate is "billing" another company to run an auction, it is vital to know the e-auction administrative cost. The team members running the auction can keep track of how long they spend on building and running the auction, which for most auctions is typically between 30 and 60 minutes. Especially once the process is established, auctions that take hours to set up and run should be rare. The cost per auctions is another place where entry-level labor benefits the business because it keeps the cost of running auctions low.

Shortly after starting our e-auction program, a company president called me with a raised voice, upset that my team was charging his business for the e-auctions we conducted. When he completed his tirade, I asked if he knew how much I had charged him. He did not; his finance team had simply told him we were cross-charging his business. I pulled up his account and found we had charged him thousands of dollars for our work based on actual hourly labor costs. Meanwhile, we reduced his RFP costs by *millions* of dollars, and he saved tens of thousands of dollars compared to his historic pricing. After that day, I sent a monthly report to the businesses I served outlining their cross-charges, their benefits from my team, and the other metrics we were tracking. Tracking metrics is one thing, but metrics truly add value when reported to stakeholders.

Comparing the e-auction result to historical pricing is a different measure than comparing it to the budget. Budget pricing can be a valuable measure to stakeholders in companies where budgeting is rigorous and calculated down to the individual commodity within the particular project. At most companies I have seen, budgets for a good or service are a guess and have only limited accountability to the overall company budget. Historical pricing is more accurate and better for answering the question, "Are e-auctions bringing us financial value?" but it is more challenging to calculate. Determining historic pricing often requires manipulating messy, difficult-to-access, and complex data. Having a spend analysis program is beyond the scope of this book but is worthwhile in answering the question of procurement value. Wherever possible, measure historical pricing and compare it to the lowest e-auction price to determine if the e-auction program benefits the company's bottom line. Whether historical pricing is adjusted for inflation is up to leadership, but most companies do not consider inflation in determining cost savings. Pricing to customers seldom tracks directly to inflation, so profit margins do not track with inflation. Actual profits, less actual costs, determine margins, and supply chains must continually measure themselves similarly.

Like the cost of running an auction, e-auction turnaround time is a simple metric to measure and is helpful for team accountability. The best way to measure it is to note the date a buyer or technical team sends each auction to the e-auction team. A more customer service-centric metric measures the date the technical team completed their evaluation. Using the technical team evaluation date is more customer service-centric because it includes the time procurement spends handing the evaluation results off to the e-auction team, which is wasted time in the technical team's view. The e-auction team then measures the turnaround as the elapsed time between the initial date and the date they send the e-auction result back to the customer. Internal transparency between these two times is critical to customer perception of the e-auction team. For example, customers of ride-sharing technology such as Uber perceive them to be faster than taxis due to the high visibility of driver status and time to completion.[1] Ride-sharing customers know exactly where their driver is when stuck at traffic lights and their estimated arrival time. The same guideline applies to the e-auction team—their internal customers will be more

---

1. Watkins, K.E., Ferris, B., Borning, A., Rutherford, G.S., Layton, D.: Where Is My Bus? Impact of mobile real-time information on the perceived and actual wait time of transit riders. Transp. Res. Part A Policy Pract. 45(8), 839–848 (2011). https://www.worldtransitresearch.info/research/3939/

patient with e-auction results if they are fully aware of the status and expected completion. While this book is limited in scope to e-auctions, an internal customer stakeholder constantly impatient with the procurement team is likely not receiving enough communication on status and expected completion date to be patient with the process.

The last key metric is based on supplier engagement. The number of invited and participating suppliers is the number of suppliers invited to bid in an auction and the number who entered bids during the process. The supplier engagement metric is essential because more suppliers qualified to bid on an e-auction improve the auction success rate and value. An example graph of this effect follows:

E-Auction Reduction vs. Qualified RFP Bidders

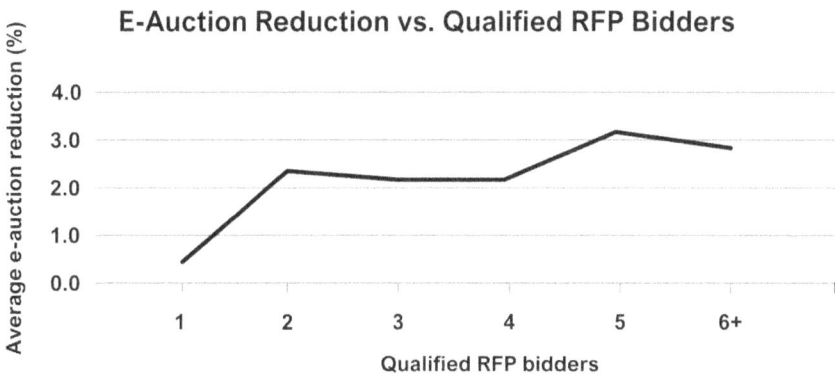

Tracking the number of invited and participating suppliers exposes issues such as technical teams disqualifying all suppliers except one, categories with particularly wide or narrow supplier pools, or categories where suppliers consistently do not participate in e-auctions. Gathering this metric allows the e-auction team to find root causes driving results and focus on improving value.

The focus of any metric, in the e-auction space or elsewhere, should be to measure something to improve or a goal to attain. If there are too many metrics, a team loses focus and spends too much time gathering metrics instead of improving the business. If there are too few metrics, a team flounders, not knowing if they are improving or adding value. Measuring the correct parameters, making those measurements visible to key stakeholders, and using them to drive results are critical to e-auction program success.

In the next chapter, we'll examine one of those key stakeholders: suppliers.

SIX

ALL ABOUT SUPPLIERS

Suppliers are one of the last stakeholder groups for buy-in but are often the most substantial opposition to an e-auction program. If you are not clear and consistent about the benefits of market data and better scopes of work, suppliers will likely see an e-auction program as purely meant to squeeze their margins. Keeping communication frequent, clear, and transparent with suppliers can strengthen the entire program because it allows them to understand *why* the company is implementing an e-auction program. Without an e-auction, suppliers often do not understand their place in the market and sometimes do not receive an opportunity to bid on work repeatedly awarded to an incumbent supplier. Also, without an e-auction, there is little reason for the technical team to write a clear scope of work to outline all work because the technical team relies on the incumbent supplier for understanding.

This chapter covers the importance of new suppliers, the logistics of supplier training, notes on how to deal with suppliers who do not participate, complacency, backsliding at the contract phase, and conducting negotiations that function similarly to e-auctions in the form of structured price comparison without a live auction component.

NEW SUPPLIERS

A core function of any supply chain team is constantly finding and refining the supplier base. While it would be easiest if the current suppliers smoothly transition to an e-auction program, some suppliers will stop supplying the company over time. The suppliers may exit because they do not participate in e-auctions, are not price competitive, or the e-auction program with clear **go/no-go criteria** better exposes their strengths and weaknesses. The reasons for exiting suppliers are in addition to the normal supplier attrition due to financial instability or shifts in market offerings. Therefore, some efforts in launching an e-auction program must be finding new entrants to key categories or carefully evaluating how to approach categories with only one or two available suppliers. The supply chain team must monitor which suppliers will struggle with an e-auction program and be ready to bring new suppliers to fill any gaps.

SUPPLIER TRAINING

The logistics of training suppliers in e-auctions is similar to any other training. It will likely involve creating how-to videos, slide presentations, and documents that follow your standard formats and are customized to your preferred software solution. The tricky part is supporting suppliers fully in a more emotional than technical transition. It will help to have a dedicated hotline suppliers can call with any questions, set hours when e-auction experts will staff this hotline, and ideally staff the hotline with the same team building the e-auctions. The staff answering this hotline will likely encounter emotional and agitated callers, so train them to keep calm and use the company's talking points. If the company already employs a call center for external customers, consider running the e-auction team through the same training as that call center. The team should use this line to call suppliers ahead of an e-auction and start to offer proactive troubleshooting and assistance if a supplier has not entered a prebid ahead of the auction start.

In February 2018, there was a heater break in our building. Moving the e-auction hotline was one of the trickiest steps in managing our scramble to use another company office during repairs. After working with our IT team, we could forward the e-auction hotline to other phone lines. The increased mobility offered by forwarding the hotline was invaluable when the COVID-19 pandemic started in March 2020, as we had already figured out how to keep this supplier hotline running. Consider contingency plans for suppliers and team members in case of expected events when you set up this infrastructure.

———

NON-PARTICIPATING SUPPLIERS

After receiving training and an invitation to the practice auction, some suppliers will refuse to participate further in the e-auction process. The most likely or stated reasons for non-participation and some potential approaches are as follows:

SUPPLIER REASON FOR NON-PARTICIPATION	POTENTIAL E-AUCTION TEAM RESPONSE
The company doesn't care about quality and is simply trying to squeeze margins	Thank you for your concern; this company values quality in all our purchases. The work scope gave the required criteria and represented the quality requirements. We have determined that you meet the quality requirements by inviting you to the e-auction. Only qualified suppliers were invited to this e-auction. If you have additional value above and beyond the scope of work, please remove those extras from your pricing and propose them as options with separate pricing.
The software is confusing and difficult to use	Thank you for your feedback. Can you tell us more about what was particularly difficult? We have created a practice auction, and we encourage you to use that to figure out how to use the system. We would be happy to set up additional practice auctions and can talk you through them on this line if that would be helpful.
We have already bid our lowest price in the RFP and cannot decrease it further	Thank you for confirming. We will use your RFP price as your auction bid. We encourage you to put that price into the auction (if the ceiling allows it) to confirm our understanding of the price you already bid. (Note to the reader: Some e-auction software allows buyers to enter proxy bids for suppliers, but others do not. If the software does not allow the company to enter bids, a low bid ceiling approach may be required to ensure the lowest auction bid wins the business and is not "outbid" by a prior lower RFP bid.)
You're simply doing e-auctions to cut costs	While e-auctions help us find the best price in the market, they also benefit suppliers. To prepare them for e-auctions, our scopes of work have to be better, and you might have already seen more complete scopes of work in our bids. The e-auction program gives you more information about where you are in the market in relation to your competitors so you can be more successful with our company and your other customers.

Some suppliers may refuse to participate despite your team's best efforts. At this point, your company needs to decide if you will entirely exit that supplier, choose not to invite that supplier to bid on work until they agree to an auction or exempt the supplier's categories from e-auction. The supplier relationship, market conditions, and category are all components of this decision and will vary from supplier to supplier. There were multiple times in my experience when a supplier would decide not to participate in e-auctions and, after not being invited to bid on work for some time, would reverse their decision.

When we started running e-auctions, three construction suppliers built wind turbine farms to harness wind energy. Two suppliers, including one pioneer for e-auctions in the early 2000s, refused to participate in any bid with an e-auction. Thanks to the convictions of our CEO, we continued with the remaining supplier. We ran their bids as single-supplier auctions for a time, much to the consternation of the wind team's leader (more can be found on single-supplier auctions in Chapter Eight). When a major wind farm project came and went, and our two non-participating suppliers were not invited to bid, they came asking about the project. Our response that their bids would be invited when they followed our e-auction policy resulted in them returning to the table. While we may have paid a little more due to a lack of competition on the first project, we saw significant savings versus historic pricing on the next two farms with all three suppliers bidding.

COMPLACENT AND BACKPEDALING SUPPLIERS

At some point in an e-auction program, suppliers can grow complacent. Suppliers typically indicate this by entering high prices at the RFP stage and then dramatically reducing pricing in the auction to win the business. The best way to combat this is only to take a few bids from RFP to e-auction, disqualifying some suppliers due to commercial requirements. The procurement team must communicate this disqualification to all suppliers when issuing the RFP and sending invites to the e-auction. Communicating the disqualification ensures the RFP pricing is reasonable without e-auction, keeping suppliers competitive.

After the auction, the procurement team must strive to cement the deal while it is fresh. Suppliers may erode their bid over time by arguing that it was entered incorrectly, noting changes in commodity prices since the bid was completed, or simply refusing to hold to the bid entered during the auction. The best defense against this erosion is to set the e-auction up for success, with the scope of work and pricing immediately formatted and ready to convert to a contract document quickly. Within an hour or two of the auction completion, the e-auction team should confirm the bid ranking and the suppliers' pricing with the best ranks. Each *day* that passes increases the risk that the supplier will back out of the e-auction result, so moving quickly to solidify that result is the best option to capture e-auction value. If suppliers refuse to honor their e-auction bid, consider moving to the second-place bidder to ensure the integrity of future e-auctions.

PSEUDO-E-AUCTIONS

A recent trend in the procurement space is a **pseudo-e-auction**. The pseudo-e-auction is a competitive bid where the buyer communicates the supplier's ranking or proximity to the lowest price. For example, the buyer would communicate to the lowest-price supplier that they are between zero and five percent above the lowest price. Other suppliers might receive feedback that they are 5–10 percent high, 10–20 percent high, 20–30 percent high, or more than 30 percent high on each item bid.

PART #	DESCRIPTION	ANNUAL USAGE	QUOTE WITH AMORTIZED TOOLING	ORDER QTY	DOMESTIC ONLY FEEDBACK	INTERNATIONAL INCLUDED FEEDBACK
510506049	WIRE HARNESS - MONITOR / LIGHT	400	194.65	25	10%-20%	10%-20%
510509798	HARNESS - LIGHT, MONITOR, NET	1160	205.23	25	>20%	>20%
628303001	HARNESS- VALVES	18	746.46	1	>20%	>20%
628304001	HARNESS- ENGINE	17	928.79	1	10%-20%	>20%
628846001	HARNESS- ENGINE	17	687.05	1	>20%	>20%
631859950	HARNESS- DASH	95	648.3	5	>20%	>20%
634537001	HARNESS- VALVE	37	619.08	1	<5%	>20%
157051001	HARNESS - AUTOFEED	616	14.83	10	<5%	>20%
163656928	HARNESS- DOM/AUST	136	96.48	5	<5%	<5%
163667604	HARNESS- FRONT	958	116.19	25	10%-20%	>20%
163667608	HARNESS- FRONT	131	195.35	5	<5%	10%-20%
163670094	HARNESS- REAR	126	204.47	5	<5%	10%-20%
163670120	HARNESS- INFEED CUMMINS	15	188.65	5	5%-10%	10%-20%
163672188	HARNESS- FRONT	287	124.41	10	5%-10%	>20%
163677002	CABLE- BATTERY 2 GA P-E, 3 LEAD	936	No Quote	25	No Quote	No Quote
180009279	HARNESS - TRAILER	290	85.78	10	<5%	<5%

Suppliers can then use this more detailed feedback to decide whether to lower their pricing or hold it in place. While this does not look or feel as much like an auction, it is very similar to a reverse e-auction. The elements of price comparison to competitors, pressure to reduce pricing, and additional market information are all present in this process. The primary difference is the time pressure component. If desired, a buyer could schedule an auction for a much longer timeframe and allow for much longer overtime to mimic this pseudo-auction process.

Supplier management is often the last component in an e-auction program, but it is as critical as internal and executive buy-in. Continually seeking new suppliers, providing adequate training and support, handling non-participating suppliers carefully, and conducting pseudo-e-auctions are all techniques to improve supplier partnership and success.

In the next chapter, we'll explore other opportunities to take your e-auction initiatives to the next level.

SEVEN
NEXT-LEVEL OPPORTUNITIES

Once the basics of an e-auction program are in place, the team has decided on standard e-auction parameters and metrics that lead to improvements, and suppliers understand the program, your e-auction team can gain further value with some next-level opportunities. Solid technical go/no-go criteria, a good scope of work, negotiated contract terms, a strategy for second and third-place suppliers, and the ability to conduct non-price auctions can all strengthen and improve an e-auction program.

GO/NO-GO CRITERIA

A key component of a good bid process is establishing clear criteria to measure and disqualify suppliers. I call these go/no-go criteria, and they represent the technical team's core needs. A well-written set of go/no-go criteria will disqualify a supplier if they fail to meet the requirements listed. If this disqualifies all supplier groups, then the scope of work will likely need adjustment to meet the industry's needs. More dangerous is when the go/no-go criteria mysteriously disqualify all suppliers except the incumbent. Disqualifying all suppliers except the incumbent indicates that the internal stakeholders do not understand or support the value of e-auctions (or even the bidding process) and are trying to manipulate the process to satisfy their desire to keep working with their incumbent supplier. If this happens, it is up to the business unit's leadership to get their team on the right path; it is *not* solely up to the procurement team to try to cajole their internal customer in the right direction.

Some poor examples of go/no-go criteria are:

- Supplier will have experience in projects like this scope of work.
- Supplier offers a 602-horsepower bulldozer.
- Supplier will be responsive to the company's requests.
- Supplier has minimal redlines to contract terms.
- Supplier has worked with the company's industry previously.

The method for writing good go/no-go criteria is similar to the one for writing reasonable goals. They should be specific, measurable, achievable, relevant, and (when applicable) time-based (SMART). The trickiest one is the "achievable" measure because that is where the criteria that disqualify new entrants tend to hide. Procurement professionals who do not know the details of the work can overlook unachievable criteria and must ask their stakeholders the right questions. Procurement teams must provide quality suppliers who can do the work, so there is often a delicate balance between qualifying enough suppliers and creating clear go/no-go criteria.

Let's rewrite the go/no-go criteria above with this in mind:

- Supplier cites two projects similar to this scope, with customer references.
- Supplier offers a bulldozer with at least a 35 cubic yard (27 cubic meters) payload.

- Supplier shall answer company email inquiries within one business day and provide a single point of contact for the company.
- Supplier offers at least a five-year warranty and a liability limitation of no less than the insurance limits in the contract terms.
- Supplier offers three references of customers in similar industries or similar regulatory environments.

Most bidding software offers the option to create questions with yes/no responses, which can provide a look at which suppliers meet the go/no-go criteria. One approach is to require these answers ahead of the entire bid due date, which offers a chance to remove or edit criteria found to be unclear, severely limiting, or irrelevant. Communicating the go/no-go criteria to suppliers is critical in the bid process because it communicates the features a company values and is willing to include in its costs. If the supplier has offerings beyond the core scope of work, those can be pulled out as options with their pricing to be added later; the competition between suppliers within the e-auction must be for the core offering. Pulling out extras and options is how the company gets to an apples-to-apples bid and uses the e-auction to its best effect.

SCOPES OF WORK

One of the most overlooked benefits of an e-auction program is its impact on the scope of work. The scope of work precisely outlines what is needed, and a clear scope of work answers the fundamental questions of what, how much, when, where, and why the company needs the material or service. When a bid process is down to the e-auction, all excess chaff must be worked out of the scope. Internal stakeholders cannot rely on their incumbent supplier to "just know" what they need. E-auctions allowing new suppliers into the mix delights procurement departments, are measured by savings and cost reductions and dismays internal stakeholders who view new suppliers as barriers to doing things the way they have always been done. The path through this inherent conflict is a clean, clear scope of work. An excellent scope of work takes time and effort; knowing the e-auction winner will be awarded the work can be a push to bring internal stakeholders to the table. When they do, procurement has to be ready to partner with, guide, and support their customer in the bid and auction process.

For a sample top-tier third-party logistics scope of work and guidelines on writing one, see the Appendix A.

CONTRACT TERMS

After the scope of work and evaluation criteria are fair and comparable and meet the core needs, contract terms are the last remaining item before the e-auction. Negotiating contracts can be long and drawn out, but completing this before the auction can speed up the process. Pushing for contract completion ahead of the e auction accomplishes two things. First, it creates a sense of urgency for completion. Second, it keeps the leverage in the hands of the company. By completing the contract before the e-auction, the suppliers are still not set on who wins the business and are more likely to make concessions on contract terms to win the work. For contracts with large or strategic suppliers, the contract team can negotiate core terms outside of any bids and then negotiate (or "wrap to") that agreement for the specific scope of work. Negotiating core terms before e-auction is especially useful for bids like capital projects where the company consistently uses a list of five to ten construction suppliers and awards various projects based on the lowest cost and best availability.

An example of the overall difference in timing between negotiating before and after e-auction is shown graphically below.

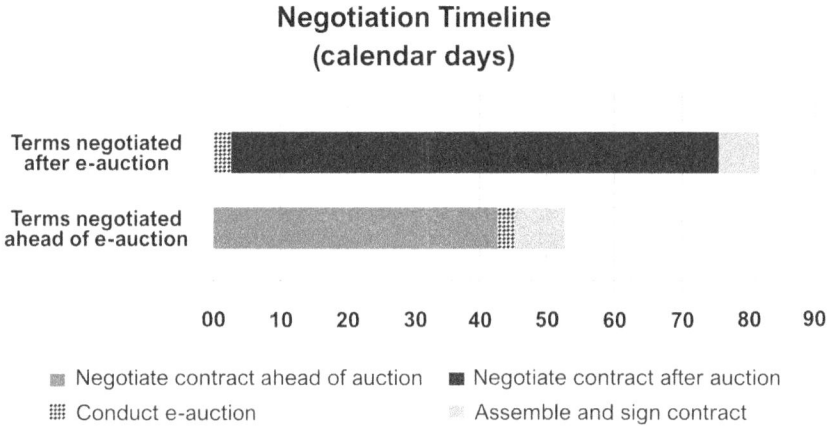

Negotiation Timeline
(calendar days)

Terms negotiated after e-auction		
Terms negotiated ahead of e-auction		

00   10   20   30   40   50   60   70   80   90

Negotiate contract ahead of auction   Negotiate contract after auction

Conduct e-auction   Assemble and sign contract

BID TRANSFORMATION

Once contract terms are negotiated (or nearly), the best practice is to quantify the risk various suppliers offer in their terms. For example, if one supplier offers a five-year warranty in their terms and another offers a seven-year warranty, there is a cost to the two extra years of risk for the first supplier. The added cost is easiest to quantify if the company has a history with the scope of work and how much the later years cost. Still, if not, the company can often estimate a reasonable failure percentage in years five through seven. Most e-auction software can then add the dollar amount determined to the supplier's bid on the company side, allowing the suppliers to compete evenly. Adding to a supplier's bid on the company side is called **bid transformation**. Let's look at an example:

The project is a capital construction project with a $1,000,000 budget. The company typically sees a failure/warranty rate of 0.5 percent each year starting in the sixth year after construction, and it goes up to a one percent failure rate each year beginning in the eighth year.

Supplier A offers a 5-year warranty and starts their bid at $995,000

Supplier B offers a 7-year warranty and starts their bid at $1,000,000

Supplier C offers a 9-year warranty and starts their bid at $1,100,000

If these suppliers were to compete on price alone, Supplier A would be the clear winner. But by adding in the total cost of ownership over 9 years, we would add $30,000 to Supplier A ($5,000 each for years 6 and 7, and $10,000 each for years 8 and 9) and $20,000 to Supplier B ($10,000 each for years 8 and 9). Their adjusted prices are as follows:

Supplier A, 5-year warranty, bids $995,000 adjusted to $1,025,000

Supplier B, 7-year warranty, bids $1,000,000 adjusted to $1,020,000

Supplier C, 9-year warranty, bids $1,100,000 adjusted to $1,100,000

Supplier B now offers the lowest total cost of ownership. The internal stakeholders prefer to work with Supplier B because they are more willing to support their work for longer, which typically increases quality. Other terms in the contract, such as insurance limits, payment terms, and even cybersecurity risk, can often be treated this way. If it can be quantified in costs, it can be included in the e-auction.

Although the conventional wisdom is to hide as much information from your negotiation partner as possible, with e-auctions, everyone benefits from transparency. Tell each supplier about their bid transformation and the reasons for that transformation. Ideally, you should do this before the contract terms are signed so the supplier can lower their "penalty" created by that risk (if desired) and compete on a more even playing field with their competitors.

SECOND AND THIRD-PLACE SUPPLIERS

After completing the contract negotiations, equalizing the contract term risks using bid transformation, disqualifying any suppliers not meeting technical criteria, and writing a clear scope of work, the last higher-level technique in an e-auction program is having a strategy for the suppliers who finish second or even third place in the auction. There are a few options on how to handle these suppliers:

- Follow up with those suppliers to verify they were not the lowest price supplier in the e-auction and that you will be working with the lowest-priced supplier without further action. Verifying without further coaching is appropriate when the bid is for something purchased frequently, when it's a smaller spend category for the company, or when there is no way to award any of the work to a secondary supplier. While post-auction follow-up is helpful for supplier relationships, you do not always need extensive discussion.

- Award a percentage of the work to the secondary or even tertiary suppliers. If some work is awarded to suppliers other than the supplier with the lowest e-auction price, communicate that this will happen *before* the auction occurs, including the percentage of work to be awarded outside the leading award. Awarding a secondary or tertiary supplier can be very powerful for building a more resilient supplier base, encouraging participation in the e-auction, and adding a comfort level to internal customers whose incumbent supplier is suddenly less competitive for price.

- Extensively coach suppliers who do not hold the lowest price at the end of the auction on their bids. During this process, ensure the confidentiality of other bidders' identities, pricing, and performance. The extensive coaching option is similar to the first option but involves more conversation and coaching to the unsuccessful bidders so they can be more successful on the next opportunity. Coaching and feedback are especially important and helpful with diverse suppliers, suppliers new to a market, and suppliers where the company is seeking a stronger relationship.

All of these options for secondary and tertiary suppliers consider the long-term goals of the supplier relationship, the category strategy, and the company's approach to managing risk.

NON-MONETARY E-AUCTIONS

Once, in a conversation with a supply chain leader, they brought up all the common objections to e-auctions: They're too impersonal, too transactional, and the leader doesn't like them. So, I asked what they were struggling with.

"Lead times are still horrible on our key commodities!" was one answer.

"Did you know you can auction lead times instead of just price?" I asked.

The contemplative look on their face said it all; they were already thinking about the applications. When I was at a large utility, we used to have projects where the large power transformer lead time was more important than its cost. Every week we saved was another week shorter for that project and another week of capacity to the grid. Our agreements with suppliers for pricing were reasonable, and we received good RFP responses that met the specifications, but we simply needed them *faster*.

So we ran an e-auction where suppliers entered bids in weeks instead of dollars. Using this method, our lead time for the transformers dropped from about 13 to 11.5 months, pushing our suppliers to reconsider their manufacturing schedule.

Lead Time Reduction Auction (weeks)

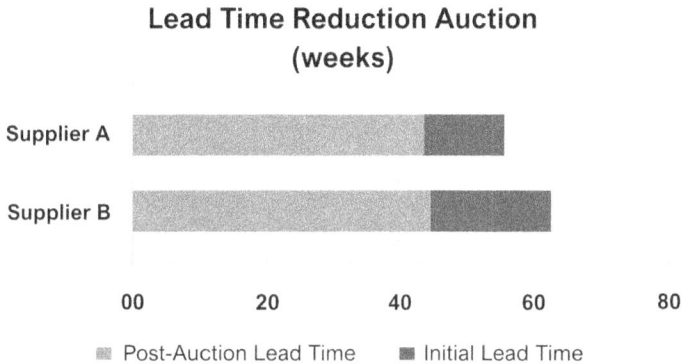

Bar chart showing lead times for Supplier A and Supplier B, with axis marks at 00, 20, 40, 60, 80. Legend: Post-Auction Lead Time, Initial Lead Time.

Clarity on the definition of lead time is required for success. When auctioning based on lead time, a company can base lead times on weeks, business days, or calendar days. The buyer must be clear about the start and end of that lead time. Is it defined as:

- Receipt of purchase order to delivery to the company's dock?
- Contract signature to shipping from the supplier's dock?
- From completion of e-auction to delivery to the third-party logistics firm?

As of this writing, **scope three emissions** are relatively new. Scope three emissions are "the result of activities from assets not owned or controlled by the reporting organization, but that the organization indirectly affects in its value chain."[1] Essentially, scope three emissions are the emissions produced by a company's suppliers and their suppliers through the supply chain until reaching the raw materials

---

1. EPA. Accessed June 5, 2024. https://www.epa.gov/climateleadership/scope-3-inventory-guidance.

production stage. Suppliers and companies are still trying to define, calculate, and report the emissions of their supply chains appropriately, as the emissions of a supplier's suppliers can be especially tricky to estimate. If a company prioritizes having suppliers reduce their scope three emissions, those commitments can be an e-auction.

Consider an auction for the target emission level by the start or end of the project/contract period. An e-auction for target emission level uses the e-auction to clarify supplier calculation requirements and define how they will be measured. A word of caution: if this is part of an e-auction, the company should consider extra time for the suppliers to prepare their bids while the topic is new in an industry. Consider making this part of the RFP response before an auction so suppliers complete the heavy lifting of calculating emissions during that bid phase.

An e-auction is a powerful negotiation tool not limited to simple material cost reductions. When the buyer focuses on the *value* they want to bring to their customer, it is a communication mechanism, clarity-adder, and transparency builder.

An entirely successful e-auction program requires a holistic approach covering go/no-go criteria, scopes of work, negotiating solid contract terms, a strong strategy for second- and third-place suppliers, and the ability to conduct non-price auctions. While an e-auction program can be successful in the short term without these elements, long-term value and sustainability come from considering all possibilities.

In our final chapter, we'll explore other angles—some of the weird ones.

EIGHT
THE WEIRD ONES

It shouldn't have surprised me how often I heard, "You can't auction that," but it did. I listened to that phrase in response to capital projects, time and equipment projects, IT services—the list went on and on. There were challenging commodities and categories to auction. Still, it always came down to the same principle: *a company can run an e-auction for anything with an apples-to-apples bottom-line number.* Common scenarios in the non-standard auction space include bids by hourly rates and set pricing for certain parts of the scope of work. This chapter also discusses the approach for e-auctions with only one bidder, categories that are truly difficult to auction, and categories that only seem difficult to auction at first glance.

HOURLY RATES

The secret to an e-auction for hourly rates is calculating a total price by calculating an estimated number of hours for a given timeframe. An annual timeframe is often the most logical and preferred based on budgets, but some bids may benefit from monthly or multiple-year timeframes. Sometimes, this means going through old invoices and receipts to develop historic hourly percentages or estimating percentages based on similar work. The following example shows this process for a job with fifty hours each week on the job site:

ROLE	PERCENT OF TIME ON THE JOB	NUMBER OF WEEKLY HOURS	HOURLY RATE	ESTIMATED COST PER WEEK	ESTIMATED COST FOR 48 ANNUAL WORKING WEEKS
Supervisor	25%	12.5	$150	$1875	$90,000
Apprentice	80%	40.0	$80	$3200	$153,600
Technical Expert	60%	30.0	$200	$6000	$288,000
Total annual estimated cost (e-auction amount):					$531,600

While this can be a good place to start, adjust the hours and percentages until the total looks reasonable to the technical team and is close to the budgeted amount. In the auction, the supplier can only change the hourly rate to keep the auction fair. It is essential to state that quantities are estimates for bidding and auction purposes and are not binding unless the company intends them as either a minimum or a not-to-exceed quantity.

The next question may be: Why not just have suppliers enter their hourly rate for each job type and add them to get a bid for the auction? This would be much simpler but makes a fundamental unspoken assumption that the supplier will bill each job title equally, leading to game-playing. To win the auction, a savvy supplier will win the bid by lowering their supervisor's hourly rate, knowing they will only bill that time for 20–40 percent of the work. Lowering only the supervisor rate lets suppliers keep their apprentice hourly rate high and still win the auction over a supplier who bills an apprentice at a lower hourly rate but a supervisor at a higher one.

The company carries the risk of an hourly rate auction, so it needs to monitor and hold suppliers accountable for working all the hours they charge and being productive during those hours. Auctioning hourly rates requires auditing and a solid supplier relationship to be cost-effective.

PROJECT COMPONENT PRICING

Setting pricing for certain parts of the scope of work becomes a project-based bid. To auction using this approach, break the service into set projects within the larger scope and decide on an award strategy. The company can then choose to award to one supplier or break apart the award based on individual projects. A best practice is to allow suppliers to bid a discounted price if they win the entire project, as shown in the following example:

CIRCUIT	NUMBER OF MILES	SUPPLIER A BID	SUPPLIER B BID	SUPPLIER C BID
Point 1 to Point 2	1000	$275,000	$270,000	$260,000
Point 3 to Point 4	806	$221,650	$250,000	$209,560
Point 5 to Point 6	730	$200,750	$211,700	$189,800
Total Bid if Supplier wins all circuits (with discount)	2536	$662,530	$658,530	$659,360

The supplier carries the risk for these unit-based bids, so they are a good choice when a company is unable or unwilling to monitor the supplier closely or when the work is very well defined.

SINGLE SUPPLIER AUCTIONS

One of the most common questions I received from internal customers was, "Why run an auction with only one supplier?" The answer to this comes back to that delicate balance between psychology and process. Suppliers do not *know* they are the only suppliers in an e-auction. Some e-auction software programs allow the buyer to decide if the suppliers can know how many suppliers are in an e-auction, and this parameter should be chosen carefully. Do not let suppliers know how many are participating, regardless of how many are invited to the event. If suppliers start to see that some RFP responses lead to auctions while others do not, they naturally ask why. Suppliers quickly see the pattern that when they are the only respondents to an RFP, there is no auction. Suppliers knowing they are the only bidder in an RFP will contribute heavily to supplier complacency, and suppliers will not bid competitively in an RFP in hopes that they do not have to refine their price in an auction. Running a single supplier auction also goes back to the bid ceiling decisions. If the buyer sets the bid ceiling at a target price (such as budget) or a little below the lowest RFP price, the supplier may still offer a reduction even as the only bidder.

Some practitioners consider single supplier auctions unethical, but they do not have to be. I agree that practitioners should not run Dutch auctions, Japanese auctions, and English Reverse auctions with no preceding RFP with one supplier. Without an e-auction program, a procurement team still typically returns to the only supplier who bids on an RFP and asks for a price refinement. Running an auction for this refinement is no different and can be less expensive in terms of labor and travel expenses for both supplier and buyer than manually negotiating. The auction serves as a double check here that the RFP price was correct, and I saw single supplier auctions reduce pricing about 10–25 percent of the time when using the low bid ceiling strategy. If the company follows this strategy, it is essential to consistently emphasize to suppliers that if they do not bid on the e-auction, their RFP price will determine the lowest bidder for the award.

NON-AUCTIONABLE AND SEEMINGLY NON-AUCTIONABLE BIDS

In dozens of conversations with my internal customers and thousands of e-auctions run by my team, we only found one for which we could not think of an auction strategy that yielded value to the company: a broker selling excess products on the open market. While I could easily auction the monthly fee or commission they charged the company, that did not capture the *value* suppliers offered. Different suppliers had access to different markets and customer groups and different track records on their ability to sell our product for the highest price.

Other purchases that came close to being non-auctionable and had multiple potential suppliers included leadership conferences, marketing services, bids with a fixed and public budget, and staff augmentation.

LEADERSHIP CONFERENCES

Leadership conferences are simple to auction if multiple venues are acceptable to the coordinating team. Simply combining the costs of food, lodging, event space, audio-visual support, and the rest of the expenses for the estimated number of attendees will yield a bottom-line number for the auction. An e-auction might be between two hotels across the street from one another, not two options across the country. However, company politics often make this difficult, as the executive and event planning teams may have strong venue preferences.

MARKETING AND CREATIVE SERVICES

The key to auctioning marketing bids or any other creative service is always getting the technical team to find multiple acceptable bidders to meet the need. Conversations ahead of the auction can evaluate supplier capabilities, review creative content, and narrow the field. Ultimately, the decision between two or three finalists can come down to the price of those services. There are times when the auction can help unite a divided set of technical panelists, some of whom prefer the look of Supplier A and some of whom prefer the look of Supplier

B. Letting both suppliers know they are technically qualified clarifies that their differentiation in the field now comes down to price.

The marketing category was not exempt from e-auction at my company, although the VP of Marketing at one of our businesses tried mightily to secure an exception. After running an RFP, completing demonstrations, and discussing extensively within the team, two suppliers remained competitive for their marketing contracts. Three marketing team members favored a new supplier, and the others favored the incumbent. The VP wanted to select one of the suppliers without an e-auction, but her business president and our CEO insisted we run one. To create an apples-to-apples bid, we e-auctioned three expected projects and estimated labor hours based on previous invoices. The e-auction resulted in a cost reduction of more than $2 million annually and hundreds of thousands of dollars in savings from the previous supplier. The incumbent supplier lowered their price below what we were currently paying, but the new supplier ultimately took the bid. They served the marketing team well over the contracted three years, and the VP of Marketing grudgingly had to admit the value e-auctions brought to her budget. I was on vacation when that e-auction ran, but receiving that phone call from my team with the auction results was the highlight of my year.

FIXED OR PUBLIC BUDGETS

For bids where the budget is fixed or public, such as the requirement to spend a certain amount due to policy or regulatory requirements, the key is to run a forward auction focusing on *benefits*. Instead of suppliers reducing their bids to win business, a forward auction is a more traditional approach where bids increase, and the highest value wins. The approach with a fixed budget is that the suppliers bid for how much benefit they can bring the company for a set cost. Companies using this approach must share the budget with suppliers, such as when a utility has a budget of $5 million to run programs to increase energy efficiency. The auction then has suppliers commit to certain levels of service. In the example given, suppliers can commit to a certain amount of energy savings for the budget. Suppliers can commit to a certain number of customer energy audits they will conduct. In another industry, the auction might be how many sales leads a supplier will provide or generate for a budget of $50,000. Or perhaps the number of customers the supplier will serve for that price. The auction is always about value, which doesn't always mean the lowest price.

STAFF AUGMENTATION

Staff augmentation, or temporary labor, has more e-auction potential than may initially appear. The staff augmentation category is a highly fractured market with many hungry suppliers interested in competing to win business. The tricky part is getting to a bottom-line number when the industry mainly focuses on markup percentages. The approach can be similar to hourly rate e-auctions as outlined previously, but the supplier is responsible for their markup percentage. The company may let suppliers enter a not-to-exceed hourly rate for each position, using the supplier's expertise in this area. Note that hourly rates depend highly on geography, so the buyer should divide the bids by geographic region.

Let's look at an example where the company sets the hourly rate:

JOB TITLE	ESTIMATED ANNUAL HOURS	EMPLOYEE HOURLY RATE	SUPPLIER MARKUP PERCENTAGE	SUPPLIER HOURLY BILL RATE	TOTAL ANNUAL ESTIMATE
Administrative Assistant	500	$18.00	16%	$20.88	$10,440
Engineer I	1040	$60.00	18%	$70.80	$76,632
Senior Engineer	600	$80.00	18%	$94.40	$56,640
Fleet Technician	800	$30.00	17%	$35.10	$28,080
Construction Apprentice	1600	$25.00	20%	$30.00	$48,000
Total annual estimated cost (e-auction amount):					$219,792

In this example, the supplier will only change the markup percentage unless they enter hourly rates. One of the most labor-intensive parts of a staff augmentation bid is gathering job descriptions for any position. Still, suppliers must be clear on the positions required. One company's "Engineer I" may be another company's "Engineering Apprentice." With staff augmentation, it is critical to include pricing for items beyond the hourly rates, including background checks, drug tests, sick leave, overtime rate, and other labor benefits. Not including these items in the bid leads to complex contract negotiations later and a low-priced supplier suddenly making up margins with huge fees.

Many categories other than materials can be tricky to bid and e-auction effectively but still hold great value. For large expenditures based on hourly rates or multi-component projects, the extra effort required to reach a bottom-line number will benefit the companies that invest that effort.

The good news is that the number of categories in which it is genuinely impossible to e-auction effectively is few and far between—all the more reason to use this tool early and often.

NINE
CONCLUSION

Many people—executive teams, procurement teams, technical teams, and suppliers—will resist e-auctions, but that's not a reason to disregard them. The old way of doing things, where suppliers and buyers would spend days or weeks wearing one another down, is simply archaic. Modern procurement teams do not have time for that dance, as they are continually asked to negotiate more spend, commodities, and savings. I have yet to see a company decide to add procurement staff and raise the required bid threshold to offload a procurement team. Instead, the opposite is usually true, and the company needs the supply chain team to find new efficiencies to cover a reduced headcount and increased workload. One source of that efficiency gain is an e-auction program, which is simply a negotiation tool at its core.

Once your company embarks on an e-auction journey and understands the process, the next step is to support the human side of program implementation. While starting with the executive team to build buy-in is intuitive, moving next to the procurement team may be less obvious. As the team members closest to the suppliers, the procurement team has the most to gain and the most to lose from a shift in how the company negotiates bids. After winning the procurement team over, the technical teams and suppliers will likely need more consistent attention and training. Both can grow weary of an e-auction program over time and will need constant support and reminders of the benefits they bring. E-auction parameters have a significant impact on the benefits all stakeholders see.

Deciding parameters such as bid ceilings, reserves, and transparency affect both benefits to the company and supplier perception of the e-auction program. Determining which categories to exempt, structuring the e-auction team, and setting metrics impact both program sustainability and internal stakeholder perception of the e-auction program. Careful use of metrics to measure actual e-auction benefits and answer stakeholder objections goes a long way toward short-term and long-term program success.

After launching an e-auction program, your company can offer higher-level opportunities. These include clear go/no-go criteria, complete scopes of work, and thoughtful contract terms. Advanced opportunities in e-auctions also include incorporating bid transformations, creating success paths for second and third-place suppliers, and considering non-monetary auctions.

Equipped with the right strategies, your company can build a successful e-auction program covering all categories and situations. Hourly rates, leadership conferences, creative services, and other "non-auctionable" categories open up when a company considers the human side of e-auctions.

The bottom line? The benefits of a well-implemented e-auction program include dramatically lowering costs, reducing cycle times, increasing information transparency, and increasing overall bid efficiency. These benefits far outweigh the costs and pitfalls and ultimately build a stronger supply chain.

SCOPE OF WORK

APPENDIX A

One of the most overlooked benefits of e-auctions is the pressure on writing a substantial scope of work. Sometimes called a statement of work, this document outlines the details of a bid for suppliers. The scope of work should outline what, how much, when, where, and why a good or service is needed. The scope of work also includes the criteria for success, and reporting requirements.

The scope of work should *not* include a massive list of questions for the supplier sales team to answer. A list like that belongs to a Request for Information, which is an entirely different process and should involve at least as much research on the buyer's part as is required of the supplier. As much as possible, the scope should not tell the suppliers how to solve the problem the company needs to solve. A good supplier base has deep expertise in their industry and will provide the most possible value if given maximum flexibility to meet requirements using whatever method they see fit. Unless there is a regulatory reason to dictate engineering methods and similar requirements, keep a scope of work focused on the results instead of the path to achieve those results.

As a buyer, I found that while I could provide a "company introduction" section of a scope and a Word document with some pretty formatting, every scope of work for complicated purchases has different needs. Instead of having a template, it is helpful to have technical teams answer a series of basic questions:

WHAT DO YOU NEED TO PURCHASE?

While this question seems obvious, it is the most logical place to start. This section is synonymous with the specification and is often fully provided by the technical team. The trick is to focus on the actual need and not what the incumbent supplier is providing, or the method the technical team thinks is required to deliver it. For example, writing a scope requesting a Caterpillar D6 bulldozer seems simple. Is that what is genuinely required? Or is there a need for equipment that can move four cubic yards of material? Or tow twenty tons off-road in rough terrain? A buyer must keep asking for the actual need until the requirement is supplier-agnostic.

HOW MUCH IS NEEDED?

Again, this seems like an intuitive place to start, but it is often overlooked. This category can include estimated annual or monthly volumes. Still, it can consist of the length of service engagement, the estimated number of hours, not-to-exceed volumes or minimums. Be clear on what is an estimate and what is set. As much as possible, make the pricing schedule or bid price reflect the value of the entire contract. If the bid is for a five-year supplier partnership on a widget that costs $5.00 with an estimated annual volume of 50,000, the bid should reflect the full value of $1.25 million and not simply $5.00. A request to bid on something worth $5.00 gets ignored, but a bid for $1.25 million does not.

WHEN SHOULD THE COMPANY TAKE DELIVERY?

When the company should take delivery of a good or service includes lead times, response times, and other timeframe-related parameters. This may be expected lead times or even how lead times will be contracted or communicated. The scope can include the lead time *if* a forecast is provided to the supplier, the maximum acceptable lead time to win the bid, or how to bid the lead time if lead times are part of the bid alongside pricing. Consider whether the lead time should be measured in weeks, days, or business days and if it should include shipping times.

For services, when something is needed might refer to the response time expected of the supplier. Does the company expect the supplier to respond within one business day? Four hours? Or perhaps the requirement is that a supplier have someone on the way to fix the equipment within a certain number of days or hours. This section also includes the length of the supplier engagement, such as the timeframe for an intensive training program.

WHERE IS IT NEEDED?

Avoid requiring a supplier to be located within a certain number of miles of the company facility if the concern is a response or lead time, which belongs in the "when" section. This is a good example of how a method of solving a problem can sneak into the requirements instead of focusing on the results. I have encountered suppliers who will be in the air at a customer's facility to solve an issue within hours, while another supplier within the same state will take days to respond. Proximity is simply not an indicator of customer service.

The section on *where* is about the good or service delivery location. Which company facility or facilities will need the goods? Is the service or training program to be delivered in person or virtually? Is the supplier expected to travel to the company for meetings or status reports? If so, what is the travel per diem or reimbursement policy, or is the supplier expected to cover the cost? The key here is to focus on the actual need for delivery and allow the supplier as much freedom as possible to meet that need. I've seen multiple instances when the supplier located farther away has better lead times than the one nearby because the farther supplier has a better logistics network.

WHY IS THE COMPANY PURCHASING SOMETHING?

Why a company needs something is an optional part of the scope of work, depending on the material or service. To reach a true supplier partnership, helping the supplier understand the *why* can help the supplier propose solutions that reduce risk and add value for both parties. For example, suppose the supplier understands how their widget is part of the overall product. In that case, they can propose an alternate material or solution at a lower cost that still meets the need. Or a services supplier who understands how the training they offer fits into existing programs can better tailor the solution to precisely what the company needs without extra frills. When including a "why" section to a scope of work, the buyer must be prepared to pivot, reissue the RFP, or otherwise modify the bid mid-flight if a supplier proposes something of excellent value that changes the scope of work. Changing the scope in light of significant changes and reissuing the RFP reestablishes a fair playing field.

WHAT CRITERIA WILL QUALIFY SUPPLIERS?

Qualification criteria are further discussed in Chapter Seven, but this is a reminder that evaluation criteria must be part of the scope of work and are the most critical part of a scope of work heading into e-auction. To improve the e-auction process, the best criteria are those with clear go/no-go or yes/no answers. *Any* no-go answer to criteria should be enough to disqualify a supplier from being able to compete in the auction, and they should be as objective as possible.

WHAT REPORTING IS NEEDED?

Reporting is how a company can hold a supplier accountable for meeting the scope. What kind of reports can the company use? At what frequency? Who receives these reports? What information do the reports need to contain? The key here is to create valuable and actionable reports that do not require too much work from the supplier. Companies often ask for lengthy reports that are too cumbersome actually to use. Keep it minimal, keep it simple, and keep it actionable.

CONTRACT LANGUAGE

A note about contract language: keep it out of the scope if there is existing language in the contract template. Examples include payment terms, maximum package weights, change notifications, etc. Because a good scope of work becomes "Exhibit A" in the contract, a conflict in terms causes legal headaches. While it is tempting to change these terms using the scope, change them in the contract documents to keep the legal requirements clean.

WHO WILL RECEIVE THE BID REQUEST?

Which suppliers the company invites to bid on a scope is an integral part of a conversation between procurement and the technical team but is not technically part of the scope of work. Multiple third-party services like Scoutbee or Tealbook can help find suppliers for particular niche needs. Consider carefully before excluding a supplier simply because a technical team had a poor experience in the past, especially if that experience is more than five years previous. For those situations, drill down to the real issue with the supplier and write the criteria and scope of work so as not to allow the same poor behavior. Examples might be that the supplier took on more work than they could handle or left a mess behind on a job site. If that unacceptable behavior is part of how that supplier does business, they will self-select or be disqualified in the technical evaluation.

Armed with this list of questions, a strong and fair scope of work is within reach. It is critical to keep communication clear between the technical team, which must use the RFP results, and the procurement team, which is expert in editing and negotiating scopes of work. In the end, it always comes down to the relationships between the technical team, procurement team, and suppliers.

Let's look at an example scope of work for a third-party logistics agreement:

EXAMPLE REQUEST FOR PROPOSAL

———

THIRD-PARTY LOGISTICS SUPPLIER

About Company

[One or two paragraphs about the company issuing the RFP, typically from marketing materials or filing reports. Include approximate company size, years in business, and industry.]

Supplier Expectations

The company expects suppliers to provide products and services that meet its specifications, quality requirements, and code of conduct.

Service Requirements

The selected supplier is expected to conduct all services professionally, according to Company instructions and agreed-to terms and conditions. All shipments shall be professionally packaged, without excess tape, on structurally sound pallets. Damage from when the supplier receives the shipment to delivery at its final destination will be the sole responsibility of the third-party logistics (3PL) supplier. The selected supplier shall provide a single point of contact for all interactions, with a backup contact when that person is out of the office and an escalation point of contact for issues.

The company is looking for an engagement in three phases and is seeking a logistics partner to grow with the business. Tentatively, Phase 1 will take place through Q3 [next year], Phase 2 will take place in Q4 [next year], and Phase 3 will start in [the year after next] upon successful engagement with Phase 1 and Phase 2.

PHASE 1: AD HOC REQUESTS

- The company will request an inbound shipment, domestic or international, and an urgency level or need-by date.
- Supplier shall respond with a price for the shipment for the Company's approval within four (4) business hours for shipments within one country and twenty-four (24) business hours for shipments between countries. Monday through Friday, business hours are considered 6:00 AM to 5:30 PM Pacific Time (GMT-8).
- Upon approval, the Supplier shall ship materials and send an Advanced Shipment Notice (ASN) to the designated Company personnel with the expected shipment arrival date and tracking information.
- For international shipments, the Supplier shall work directly with the international shipper to expedite material through customs. The company shall promptly facilitate or provide the necessary paperwork to move material through customs.
- For non-expedited shipments, the Supplier shall combine shipments whenever possible to increase the number of full truckloads and decrease the shipping cost per pound. If combining shipments results in a delivery date more than one business day after the need-by date, the Supplier shall seek

written approval from an authorized supply chain team member to combine and deliver late.

- Supplier shall give Company access to freight tracking and storage software without additional charges to track its shipments.

PHASE 2: SUPPLIER COLLECTS SHIPPING, SHIPPING COMPLETED TRUCKS AND BONDED WAREHOUSE

- This includes all activities and requirements in Phase 1 and the requirements below.
- The 3PL Supplier shall work with the Company's other suppliers to ship materials, collect, cover and coordinate all shipments from those suppliers for billing to the Company. The company will refer its suppliers to the 3PL supplier for direct shipment coordination.
- Supplier shall maintain a bonded warehouse within the U.S. at a location mutually agreed upon between Company and Supplier. The most likely location is between Chicago, Indianapolis, or Columbus. The warehouse cost to the Company shall include all rent, racking, forklift rental, labor, cycle counting costs, etc., to run the warehouse with no additional fees or charges.

PHASE 3: CROSS-DOCKING

- Includes all activities and requirements in Phase 1 and Phase 2, but at reduced volumes when replaced with procedures from Phase 3.
- Receiving charges will be per pallet for partial truckloads, including unloading, putting away, rearranging, pallet disposal, and any other handling to warehouse the material.

- The supplier shall place materials orders with Company suppliers and charge as a percentage of the purchase order value. The supplier shall handle all shipping and customs to its warehouse and combine shipments wherever possible. The supplier may charge Company shipping costs according to the same guidelines as Phase 1 and Phase 2.
- The company shall place orders with the chosen supplier directly, which will be delivered to the requested location as a bundle kitted per machine or week of production. The supplier shall calculate fees to kit bundles and ship twice a month.
- Supplier shall ship a full truckload weekly to any Company production facility needing regular shipments at a fixed weekly rate. The price for the fixed weekly rate shall include packaging and loading.
- Suppliers shall carry insurance to cover the product's value within the warehouse. Insurance costs shall be included in the other fees charged to the Company.

The company shall provide at least 30 days' written notice between Phase 1 and Phase 2 and at least 90 days' written notice between Phase 2 and Phase 3.

———

VOLUMES

These quantities are for estimation purposes only and do not guarantee volumes or business.

Phase 1

- For the first half of next year, approximately 2-3 inbound shipments per week.

- For the second half of next year, approximately 4-5 inbound shipments per week.

Phase 2

- Outbound shipping approximately five completed products per week in the second half of next year and up to 20 trucks per week in the year after next.

Phase 3

- Six weeks' inventory=estimated 1,100 pallets at the end of next year (30,000 square feet), increasing to 1,900 pallets in the year after next (48,000 square feet).
- Approximately $70m is spent on purchase orders per year in the year after next.
- In the year following, approximately eight machines per week will be produced on the east coast of the US and approximately 12 machines per week in the Midwest US.

Supplier Code of Conduct

The supplier code of conduct requires suppliers to meet the highest employee safety and health standards, ethical and legal requirements, human dignity, and labor standards, including actively removing forced and child labor from its supply chain, securing the Company's data and intellectual property, and meeting the highest environmental and stewardship standards. The company expects suppliers to be transparent about efforts to meet the code of conduct and plans to improve results in this area continuously.

———

REPORTING

Supplier shall provide a monthly report to Company supply chain personnel, including a minimum of the following:

Phase 1

- The average rate per pound for freight is separated into two categories: hazardous materials / dangerous goods and other materials.
- Percentage of shipments sent as standard route / milk run, full truckload, and partial truckload.
- Percentage of shipments expedited (air vs. ocean freight, team transported, etc.) and additional cost incurred by expediting.
- Comparison of rate paid to spot rates in the same period, where an independent third party backs the spot rate data.
- The on-time delivery percentage for inbound shipments (compared to ASN expected delivery date and requested initially by date).

Phase 2

- All reporting requirements of Phase 1.
- On-time delivery percentage for outbound completed vehicles.
- Percentage usage of the warehouse space.

Phase 3

- All reporting requirements of Phase 1 and Phase 2
- Average cost to Company per purchase order placed.
- The number of pallets unloaded and loaded each month.
- Percentage of material cycle counted each month by volume.

SAMPLE E-AUCTION PROGRAM IMPLEMENTATION PLAN
APPENDIX B

The following table is an example program plan for implementing e-auctions. This assumes you have already gathered executive support and are running sourcing events (RFXs) using the planned sourcing software to be used for e-auctions. The plan below also assumes the company has identified the employees who will serve in a few key roles. One employee may hold multiple roles on the team, and the key roles include:

- **Procurement Leader** - The Procurement Leader is sufficiently high in the organization to make decisions about policy and procurement processes regarding e-auctions. This role may be the direct manager for the E-auction Leader.
- **E-auction Leader** - The E-auction Leader is the effective leader of the e-auction team and the first escalation point for questions about e-auctions and the process. They should have read this book and potentially conducted some additional research if e-auctions are new to them. In the plan below, there are times the e-auction team might be substituted for the E-

auction Leader depending on their level of training and comfort with e-auctions.

- **Project Manager** - The Project Manager role ensures the e-auction implementation project is going according to schedule and coordinates the activities of all other roles in the plan. It is typical for a Project Manager to be outside of the core e-auction team in order to continue to push schedules and activities with a more third-party perspective.

- **Category Managers** - The Category Managers are the procurement team members with ultimate jurisdiction over the purchased categories. The Category Managers or their team members are conducting the RFXs, managing the suppliers, talking to technical teams, editing scopes of work, and setting category strategies. The Category Managers are the key procurement team members to which the e-auction team is passing e-auction information and results.

- **Software Admin** - The Software Admin has administrative access to the sourcing software and is the escalation point for software issues. They have the ability to grant software permissions to the E-auction Leader and team members and may or may not be within the supply chain or procurement team.

- **Process Expert** - The Process Expert is responsible for documenting, establishing, and improving processes within the procurement team. This role is the most likely to overlap one of the other roles and is important in creating efficient and sustainable processes so the e-auction team maintains momentum and continues to show value over time.

- **Change Manager** - The Change Manager is in charge of the change management process, including communication with stakeholders inside and outside procurement. This employee may be from another team in the company focused on change management or may be from within procurement.

TASK	WHO	WEEK START	WEEK END	1	2	3	4	5	6	7	8	9	10	11	12	13	14	15	16	17
Draft implementation plan	Project Manager	1	2	X	X															
Meet with sourcing software for training and capability check	Software Admin	1	2	X	X															
Initial walkthrough of sourcing software platform	Software Admin	2	2		X															
Understand the step by step requirements from sourcing software from a system perspective	Process expert	2	2		X															
Establish e-auction procurement center of excellence	E-auction leader	2	3		X	X														
Complete implementation plan	Project Manager	2	3		X	X														
Allocate existing e-auction personnel resources	Procurement leader	2	3		X	X														
Develop internal key business unit stakeholders & supplier communications and training plan	E-auction leader	2	4		X	X	X													
Determine and document the standard process for each 'part' of the e-auction process	Process expert	2	3		X	X														
Collaborate with the change management team to create a change management plan	Change manager	3	4			X	X													
Understand end to end process for e-auction activity	Process expert	3	5			X	X	X												
Create procurement e-auction templates	E-auction leader	3	5			X	X	X												
Identify pilot primary and secondary pilot categories	E-auction leader	4	5				X	X												
Identify "quick win" categories for first e-auctions - small, fast, well-defined materials	E-auction leader	4	5				X	X												
Create procurement training	E-auction leader	5	6					X	X											
Conduct technical team stakeholder discussions	Category Managers	5	36					X	X	X	X	X	X	X	X	X	X	X	X	X >>
Hire e-auction team	Procurement leader	6	10						X	X	X	X	X							
Deliver procurement team training	E-auction leader	6	7						X	X										
Procurement team workshops and Q&A sessions	E-auction leader	6	7						X	X										
Understand where the stakeholders are in terms of the change (for, against, neutral)	Change manager	6	7						X	X										
Determine level of engagement required to make the change with the stakeholders and suppliers	Change manager	6	7						X	X										
Phase I: Identify ten key opportunities in initial category	Procurement leader	7	8							X	X									
Phase I: Identify three key opportunities in secondary category	Procurement leader	7	8							X	X									

TRANSFORM PROCUREMENT

TASK	WHO	WEEK START	WEEK END	1	2	3	4	5	6	7	8	9	10	11	12	13	14	15	16	17
Create supplier training	E-auction leader	7	8							X	X									
Establish e-auction metrics and reporting cadence	E-auction leader	7	8							X	X									
Identify internal stakeholder & suppliers of initial categories	Category Managers	8	8								X									
Identify potentially difficult suppliers and internal stakeholders	Procurement leader	8	36								X	X	X	X	X	X	X	X	X	>>
Phase I: Gather information in Phase I categories for e-auctions to execute	Category Managers	8	9								X	X								
Communicate plan with technical team for Phase I categories	Category Managers	8	9								X	X								
Train suppliers in e-Auctions (ahead of e-Auction)	E-auction leader	9	10									X	X							
Run first e-auction	E-auction leader	9	9									X								
Conduct post-auction analysis, takeaways, and feedback	E-auction leader	9	10									X	X							
Refine e-auction template and training (supplier, procurement, etc.)	E-auction leader	9	14									X	X	X	X	X	X			
Phase II: Select next ten specific opportunties for e-auction	Project Manager	10	11										X	X						
Conduct Phase I e-auctions	E-auction leader	10	14										X	X	X	X	X			
Celebrate early wins	E-auction leader	10	11										X	X						
Deliver e-auction team training	E-auction leader	11	11											X						
Determine e-Auction exceptions	Procurement leader	11	12											X	X					
Phase II: Gather information in Phase II categories for e-auctions to execute	Change manager	11	12											X	X					
Establish 12 month e-auction schedule based on sourcing schedule	E-auction leader	11	13											X	X	X				
Communicate plan with technical team for Phase II categories	Category Managers	12	13												X	X				
Edit procurement policy and procedures	Procurement leader	12	14												X	X	X			
Conduct Phase II e-auctions	E-auction leader	13	16													X	X	X	X	
Repeat steps for Phase II until all intended categories are included in the e-auction program	E-auction leader	14	36														X	X	X	>>
Identify and implement continuous improvement mechanisms	E-auction leader	15	22															X	X	>>

GLOSSARY

All of these definitions refer to how the terms are used in this book. There may or may not be alternate usages or nuances found in other contexts.

Apples-to-apples - the comparison of two or more items that are similar enough to have an even comparison. The items being compared do not need to be identical, but the buyer must reconcile or account for their differences.

Auction transparency - the information visible to bidders in an e-auction.

Best and final offer - the last step in a negotiation process where a buyer calls for suppliers to refine their offering as much as possible. An e-auction is a possible method to conduct a best and final offer process.

Bid - a supplier's offering to a buyer, generally originating from an e-auction or RFX process.

Bid ceiling - the highest possible bid a bidder can enter in a reverse e-auction.

Bid cycle - the period of time between bids for a given category. A bid cycle might be predetermined, such as based on a contract expiration date, or it might be ad hoc when needed due to a change in the market.

Bid decrement - the amount by which a bidder has to improve from their previous bid for the new bid to be accepted. Can be a percentage or a set amount depending on the software capabilities.

Bid transformation - modifying a supplier's bid on the buyer side to adjust for costs outside of the supplier's control. This might include transition costs to change suppliers, differences in contract terms, or the cost of additional lead times. Not all software programs allow for e-auction bid transformation.

Bidder - a supplier participating in an RFX, bid, or e-auction process.

Buyer - a representative of a company or a company looking to purchase a good or service in the market. A buyer is both an individual title or role and any business or company seeking to purchase from the supplier market.

Category - a group of goods or services for purchasing, used to classify purchasing expenditures. Procurement teams are often organized by category.

Cost reduction - in the context of e-auctions, the difference between the lowest RFP bid (or starting e-auction bid in straight-to-auction events) and the ending e-auction bid.

Dutch reverse auction - an e-auction where bids start low and increase at set time intervals. The first supplier willing to enter the auction at the current bid amount wins the auction.

E-auctions - an online process by which participants bid up or down on an offering. In this book, e-auctions generally refer to reverse English auctions where suppliers are decreasing their bids to a buyer until they reach their lowest available offering, increasing the buyer's value through the course of the auction.

E-auction team - the team of people dedicated to conducting e-auctions for a company.

Emissions - measurement of the waste created by a business. Scope 1 emissions refer to the sources of waste that come directly from an organization, such as burning fuel in a company's fleet vehicles. Scope 2 emissions refer to waste a company generates indirectly, such as from purchasing electricity to run plants or other buildings. Scope 3 emissions refer to the waste created by the suppliers for a business, and are the typical focus for a supply chain.

English reverse auction (or reverse English auction) - an e-auction where the participants bid down on the offering over a set period of time. Often includes overtime so the e-auction does not end until all participants are done bidding.

Executives (or Executive team) - the leadership team for a company, typically composed of the CEO or President and their direct reports. At some companies, there may be a certain job title such as vice president or senior director considered to be part of the executive team.

Forward auction - auction where the bidders increase their bids through the course of the auction, is the opposite of a reverse auction.

Go/No-go criteria - binary criteria established in a scope of work that determine if a supplier is qualified to provide the requested good or service. The only possible responses to go/no-go criteria are "yes, the supplier meets this criteria" or "no, the supplier does not meet this criteria."

Historical price - the price previously paid for a good or service. Typically used to calculate savings.

Incumbent (or incumbent supplier) - the current supplier providing the good or service to a company, in contrast to a new or alternate supplier.

Internal customer - see "Technical Team."

Japanese reverse auction - an e-auction where the bid decreases over time at set intervals and suppliers choose to stay in the auction at the current bid or exit the auction. The last supplier to be in the auction wins the bid.

Lead time - the time between when a buyer sends a purchase order to when the supplier ships a product or the buyer receives that product. Which timing is used to determine lead time is based on contract terms between buyer and supplier.

Live auction (or live e-auction) - the e-auction that is binding on both buyer and supplier for the good or service purchased. In contrast with the practice auction, which is non-binding.

Overtime - the extension of an e-auction past its original intended end.

Practice auction (or practice e-auction) - a non-binding auction used for training purposes with a supplier. A practice auction provides a space to learn the e-auction system and its rules, understand the setup, and provide a hands-on learning tool ahead of the live e-auction.

Procurement - the component of a supply chain that focuses on sourcing/bidding, supplier management, and cutting purchase orders. Also refers to the team of people responsible for the procurement function.

Pseudo-e-auction - a feedback round that imitates an e-auction by communicating a supplier's rank or proximity to the lowest bid. Is typically a slower process than an e-auction.

Reserve price - a price at which the auction is non-binding on the auctioneer, regardless of auction activity. For a reverse auction, if the bids do not go below the reserve price, the auction is invalid. For a forward auction, if the bids do not go above the reserve price, the auction is invalid. The reserve price may be hidden or visible depending on auction settings, but is typically hidden.

Reverse auction - auction where the bidders reduce their bids through the course of the auction, is the opposite of a forward auction.

RFX - Request for X, where X represents a proposal (RFP), quote (RFQ), information (RFI) or any number of items requested by a buyer to suppliers. An RFP process is also referred to as a tender process in some parts of the world.

Savings - the reduction in costs for purchasing a good or service. The definition of savings versus cost avoidance varies between companies.

Scope of Work (or SOW) - a document outlining the buyer's needs from the marketplace, including the specification, quantity, location, delivery method, reporting, bid criteria, and any additional information.

Sourcing software - software used to connect buyers and suppliers to facilitate the process of purchasing goods and services. Sourcing software is typically hosted by the sourcing software supplier (software-as-a-service or SAAS) and paid for by the buyer.

Spend - the expenditures by a company in the marketplace over a given period of time (typically one year).

Straight-to-auction - an e-auction run without a preceding RFX or bid process.

Supplier - a company looking to sell a good or service in the market, the counterpart to a buyer.

Supply chain - both the value stream of goods and services purchased by a company and the team of people who manage that flow of goods and services. Components of a supply chain include procurement, logistics, and warehousing.

Technical team - the group of people within a company who will be using the goods or services purchased from the supplier. This group is responsible for the specification and scope of work as they are accountable for knowing what is needed to perform their work.

Ties - when one or more bidders enter the same bid.

ACKNOWLEDGMENTS

In August 2019, Stephanie Kitchen told me I should write a book about e-auctions. When I countered that I didn't know if I had enough information to fill a book, she texted me an outline of ten chapter titles and one-sentence summaries. Thank you, Stephanie, for getting me started and for your unwavering faith that I could write this book.

Thank you to my husband, Ryan Marquardt, for always standing by me, quietly keeping my water glass full while I'm writing or working, and the office door closed when the cats, children, or Roomba were too loud.

Thank you to my father, John Gustafson, for being my first reader and editor. Your thoughts and questioning of my supply chain jargon were valuable in adding clarity to this book, especially as a non-supply chain practitioner.

Thank you to LoAnn Campbell, my English teacher, for teaching me how to write. Every writer who gets this far has at least one teacher who helps them hone their craft; you were mine.

Thank you to Dennis Teel for being the kind of person whose response to "You can't do that" is, "Oh yeah? Watch me." You were my bridge into procurement and supply chain, and I'm so happy I'm here. You also taught me through example to ignore the haters because they will never appreciate me for what I can do.

Thank you to my e-auction team members, especially Clarke Grandquist. Clarke, you and I had to wander around in the dark together, and your colossal patience and persistence got us through many tough conversations. Grant Suttie, Grant Crowell, Kristina Nixson, Jose Blanco, Andrew Cerven, Tonya Williams, Angela Gust, and Dev Padavath, you all brought something to that first e-auction program. You won battles I didn't even know you fought.

Thank you to Joe Moore (Joseph Francis Moore IV, if we're being formal) for your unshakeable faith and support for a young Director who had no idea what she was doing. You were everything I needed in a leader on this e-auction journey and beyond, and I wouldn't trade our Saturday morning strategy sessions for anything.

Finally, thank you to the professional editing team who made this book a reality. Jessica Burdg, your early guidance and edits focused and honed the direction of this book beautifully. Sierra Melcher, Erika Hull, and the rest of the team at Red Thread Books thank you for the community, guidance, and sheer get-it-done power that resulted in this project's completion.

ABOUT THE AUTHOR

Image Credit: Jayme Peters, Storyteller Collective Photo Co

Like many supply chain professionals, Janice Marquardt never planned to be in procurement. She was an engineer, and that second major in communication studies was there just for balance. When she needed a graceful way out of a political career situation, she found herself in a role as an Engineering Buyer and also found her calling. From there, Janice became a commodity manager and then moved to a senior buyer role at a large utility company. Over nine years, she moved into Procurement Manager, Director of Global Procurement, and then Vice President of Supply Chain roles, including building teams and processes using her engineering problem-solving skills. She lives on a farm west of Des Moines, Iowa, with her husband, two children, one great Pyrenees dog, three cats, two dozen Belted Galloway "Oreo" cows, and about 40 chickens.

Janice founded Passwall Solutions in 2023. The company focuses on solving supply chain problems and helping supply chain teams create and capture value. Passwall Solutions has helped multiple clients elevate their procurement teams from simply cutting POs to truly strategic sourcing and has guided multi-billion-dollar e-auction program implementations. Janice can be reached on LinkedIn, at Janice@passwallsolutions.com or her website.

www.passwallsolutions.com

in linkedin.com/in/janice-marquardt-28924a8

Passwall
S O L U T I O N S

E-auction Program Results by Week
Data from actual Passwall Solutions Client

Events ——Cost Reduction ($m)

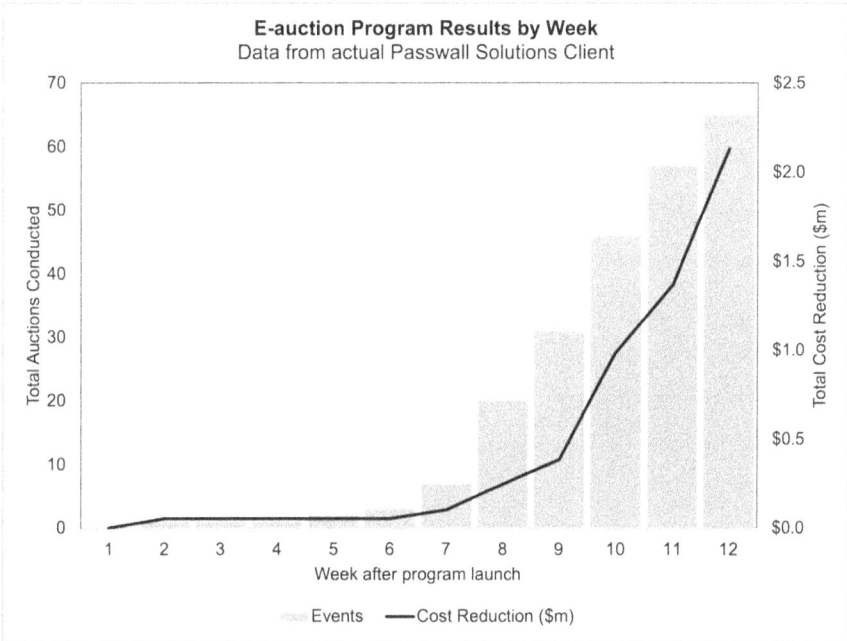

Work With Janice

Accelerate your e-auction program with real results in 8-12 weeks from launch with custom hands-on expertise and support. Or order copies of this book for your whole team to build buy-in from the start.

Contact her directly at
Janice@passwallsolutions.com
to learn more or order multiple copies

RED FALCON PRESS

CULTIVATE · ELEVATE · INNOVATE

Publish with Red Falcon Press, an imprint of Red Thread Publishing.

We provide expert guidance to nonfiction authors through every stage of the publishing process. Visit **www.redthreadbooks.com** to learn more and connect with our team.

REVIEW THIS BOOK

Enjoyed *Transform Procurement*? Your feedback means the world! If the book resonated with you, inspired you, or offered something meaningful, we'd truly appreciate it if you left a review. Your feedback helps others discover the book—and it directly supports the author's work.